Heritage Walks in the Peak District

Clive Price

Published by Sigma Leisure – an imprint of
Sigma Press, 1 South Oak Lane, Wilmslow, Cheshire SK9 6AR, England.

British Library Cataloguing in Publication Data
A CIP record for this book is available from the British Library.

ISBN: 1-85058-329-3

Typesetting and Design by: Sigma Press, Wilmslow, Cheshire.

Maps by: Orbit Design

Text photographs: by the author, except where indicated

Cover photograph: Peveril Castle, Castleton (by permission, Emglish Heritage)

Printed & bound by: Manchester Free Press, Longford Trading Estate, Thomas Street, Stretford, Manchester M32 0JT.   Tel: 061-864 4540

General Disclaimer

Whilst every effort has been made to ensure that the information given in this book is correct, neither the publisher nor the author accept any responsibility for any inaccuracy.

Preface

My first experience of real walking was gained on the moorlands immediately to the west of Sheffield, especially in the area bounded by the Rivelin Valley, Moscar Heights, Hathersage and Grindleford. Gradually my horizons were widened by outings onto the Derwent Edges, Kinder Scout and Bleaklow, followed by trips into the gentler environment of the White Peak. Later residence on the western side of the Peak District, opened-up areas around Glossop, Hayfield, the Goyt Valley and Macclesfield Forest, to say nothing of the Roaches, Dovedale and the Manifold Valley.

This intimacy with the Peak District proved to be the springboard for a lifetime's enjoyment of walking further afield, both in this country and abroad. Yet, living close to the National Park, I return there frequently and time has not eroded my enthusiasm. It is this enthusiasm I wish to share with all who read this book. The Peak District contains a wide variety of landscape and, in the course of preparing this collection of walks, even I have discovered new corners which have given me great pleasure.

One problem it has not solved. I still cannot decide whether, in general, I prefer the Dark Peak to the White. There are days when I think it is one, days when I am certain it is the other. Perhaps it will never be solved . . . to my satisfaction at least. But then that is the lure of the Peak District.

I must thank Graham Beech for all his guidance and help in the preparation of this book and also the staffs of the libraries in Manchester, Sheffield, Derby and Macclesfield for their assistance. Finally my gratitude to the members of my family for their encouragement and also to Tamsin for accompanying me on occasions.

Clive Price

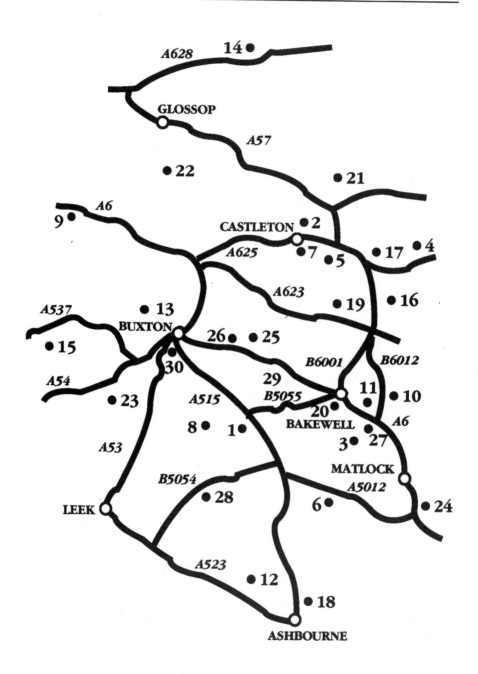

CONTENTS

The Walks

Introduction

Initially, it is the scenery which attracts visitors to the Peak District National Park. The peat, heather-covered moors with their gritstone edges and rock outcrops weathered into weird shapes, enclose the northern moors in a great horseshoe from Curbar and Baslow in the east to Leek in the west.

To the south the extensive limestone plateau is segmented by steep-sided valleys long renowned for their beauty. Dovedale, the Manifold Valley, Lathkill Dale, Bradford Dale, Chee Dale and many others of lesser fame, all offer a lusher environment than the grim, often forbidding moorlands of Bleaklow, Kinder Scout and Black Hill.

Contrary to appearances, none of this is true wilderness. The peat bogs of the moorlands are testimony to the fact that once trees flourished there. In recent years scientific experiments and soil analysis have confirmed this.

Climate, weathering and man have all combined to fashion the landscape that we know and admire today.

In this collection of walks we are concerned with the impact of man from the day he wielded a primitive stone axe to start the forest clearances to more modern times when he harnessed the fast flowing streams and rivers to spawn the Industrial Revolution. Farming, lead mining, quarrying and other industries run like threads through the history of the area. Others flourished but briefly.

As in other parts of Britain, the Romans left their mark while, in the Middle Ages, kings and barons constructed their castles. In later centuries these gave way to the impressive and often elegant mansions of the aristocracy which now attract tourists by their thousands.

The Church, too, bequeathed a legacy of Saxon crosses, tiny chapels and great churches although, within the national park, there are no remains of either great cathedrals or abbeys. The closest is Tideswell parish church, often referred to as "the Cathedral of the Peak". However, the number of 'granges' scattered amongst the farm names of the White Peak still provide living proof that monastic houses from other areas exerted a strong influence on sheep farming.

Industrial activity generates communications and the Peak District is not deficient in this respect. Today it is possible to trace ancient trackways, Roman roads, packhorse routes and turnpike roads. Most, if not all these walks, follow in the footsteps of our ancestors.

The aim of these walks is to lead the rambler not merely through some of the most exhilarating and beautiful scenery these islands have to offer but to enable him or her to explore the rich and varied tapestry that is the heritage our forbears left behind.

Each walk is based primarily on one focal point, whether it be at the start of the walk or in the middle of the route, but it is impossible to wander through this countryside without finding other points of interest. Details of these have been incorporated as well.

All the routes are circular on the assumption that most people travel by car. However, for those who prefer to use public transport details of rail and bus travel where applicable are given at the start of each route. Do remember that time-tables change so consult the telephone numbers given below.

If you enjoy these walks as much as I have in researching them, I shall be amply rewarded.

Transport Enquiries

Rail Services: 061 228 2331
Buslines: Derby 0332 292200; Buxton: 0298 23098;
          Chesterfield 0246 250450
National Express: 061 228 3881

Clothing & Safety

Many of the paths and tracks utilised in these walks are rocky or muddy or both. Stout footwear, preferably walking boots with a good grip, is essential. Even on level ground it is possible to twist or sprain an ankle. Obviously a small first-aid kit should be carried at all times. Even a minor scratch caused by barbed wire should be treated because of the risk of infection.

The walker should be equipped with waterproofs in view of our fickle climate. Remember that a fine warm day can end with lower temperatures, so extra clothing should be carried. Some of these walks venture onto high ground which also means a fall in temperature. For extra security, especially as mist descends, a compass and a knowledge of how to use it is invaluable. In case of accidents and the need to summon help, a whistle is an obligatory aid.

In addition to any meals carried, emergency rations should be found in all walkers' rucksacks. Even a bar of chocolate is better than nothing.

While I hope you will find the route instructions clear and concise it is also advisable to carry the appropriate Ordnance Survey map. Always leave word with a friend or a note in the car to say where you plan to walk. In case of emergency the Mountain Rescue Team will be able to find you more quickly.

Courtesy

Remember that the Peak District, although a National Park, is still a living and working environment. Farmers, landowners and others employed there will welcome your co-operation in closing gates, staying on paths, respecting their privacy, not causing obstructions by thoughtless parking and by taking all your litter home. Most of them will respect your right to walk in the countryside: respect their's to work and live there.

You will also find that many of them will welcome a greeting and a few words of friendly conversation. In this way you may learn facts that no book contains. Some of the information contained in these pages has been gleaned in this fashion.

1. Arbor Low

There is a concessionary footpath to Arbor Low and Gib Hill from the Parsley Hay to Youlgreave road. Otherwise there are no paths in the immediate vicinity. Therefore a visit to Arbor Low has been combined with an easy, level route starting from Parsley Hay which is about one mile away.

Route: Parsley Hay – High Peak Trail – Blakemoor – Hartington Station – Hartington Moor – Parsley Hay.

Distance: 5 miles.

Start: Parsley Hay car park, signed from the A515 between Buxton and Newhaven. Map Reference 637146.

Map: "The Peak District, White Peak Area", Number 24 in the Ordnance Survey's Outdoor Leisure series.

Public Transport: Buses from Buxton on Saturdays and Sundays. Buses from Glossop, Huddersfield, Ashbourne, Mansfield and Macclesfield on summer Sundays and Bank Holidays.

Car: Parsley Hay car park is signed from the A515 between Buxton and Newhaven.

Refreshments: There is a drinks machine and confectionery counter at Parsley Hay. A mobile caterer serves drinks and light meals at Hartington station.

The "Jug and Glass" pub, 100 yards off the route, serves bar meals at midday and in the evening.

Arbor Low and Gibb Hill

Arbor Low is one of the most important henge sites in England, often being referred to as "The Stonehenge of the North". It is located in the centre of a large, windswept plateau and, given certain types of gloomy weather, can evoke an eerie, awesome atmosphere.

Arbor Low Stone Circle

Excavations have revealed that it was built about 2,000 years B.C. by the Beaker folk who lived between the Neolithic and Bronze Ages. Controversy rages round its function but the generally accepted theory is that it was a tribal gathering ground and used for sun worship.

It is almost 300 feet in diameter surrounded by an earthwork bank and ditch. Not all the original stones remain but there are 39, all but one recumbent on the ground. Originally they would have stood upright. About 350 yards away is Gib Hill. Excavations have shown that this was constructed in two different periods. Originally a mound was built for the performance of some fertility rites, probably for crops. This has been proved by the discovery of animal bones covered with hazel twigs and flints. During the Bronze Age a burial mound was placed on top.

The Walk

Leave the car park in a southerly direction, heading along the signed High Peak Trail towards Friden and Cromford. After half a mile, at a junction recognised by a sign carved into a concrete base, the Tissington Trail branches away to the right.

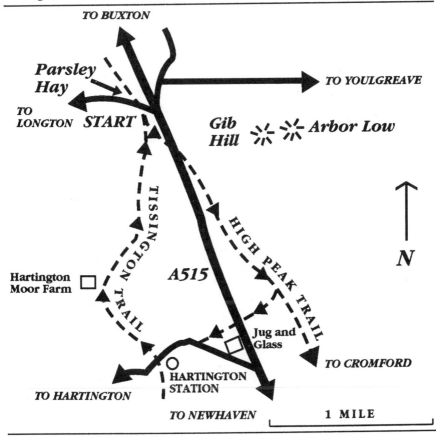

Ignore this by forking left, still with the High Peak Trail. In late summer and early autumn look for large numbers of snails in the flanking vegetation. They sport yellowish-green shells circled by brown bands.

Continue through Blakemoor cutting, now a nature reserve managed by the Derbyshire Wildlife Trust. Because it is limestone country this is rich in flora, some of it rare but also including commoner varieties ranging from scabious to harebell. The rosebay willowherb was probably brought in during the railway era because an alternative name for it is "fireweed". It has a tendency to colonise burned ground.

Passing under the first bridge, which carries the A515, look up to see the coat of arms of the Cromford and High Peak Railway Company which was formed in 1826. The bridge also carries the name of Joseph Jessop, the engineer responsible for planning the railway and also for its construction.

Beyond a second bridge there are several railway artefacts to be seen including an old signal post minus its semaphore arm and also a gradient post. Pass through a small gate alongside a five-barred one, cross a lane to a second gate and continue along the trail. Notice the patches of heather here because they are unusual in this area of the Peak District.

Hartington Signal Box, now an Information Centre

After passing through Blakemoor plantation, a broadleaved woodland in which beech predominates, another small gate is reached adjacent to another five-barred one. Pass through and immediately turn right to climb along a wide walled lane. On reaching the A515 cross with extreme caution into another lane directly opposite. The "Jug and Glass" is 100 yards to the left.

The lane stays level for a distance before dropping downhill to meet the B5054. Turn right down the road but, after 350 yards and by a small disused lime kiln, turn left up the signed approach to Hartington Station. At the top of the slope, by the signal box which is now used by the National Park as an Information Centre, turn right onto the Tissington Trail, now heading northwards.

Pass through several cuttings where the summer flora produces a blaze of colour. Between these cuttings the trail affords some extensive views over the White Peak, especially to the left where Carder Low, Chrome Hill and Long Dale are all visible on a clear day.

Beyond the impressive stone buildings of Hartington Moor Farm the line sweeps round in a semi-circle before entering Parsley Hay cutting, now another nature reserve. Beyond, the Tissington Trail re-joins the High Peak for the final half mile back to the starting point.

2. Mam Tor

A moderate walk using both field paths and moorland tracks. One severe climb is rewarded by splendid views over both the Dark and White Peaks.

Route: Edale – Barber Booth – Chapel Gate – Rushup Edge – Mam Tor- Hollin's Cross – Edale

Distance: 6 1/2 miles.

Start: Car Park, Edale. Map reference 125853

Map: "The Peak District, Dark Peak Area", Number 1 in the Ordnance Survey's Outdoor Leisure series.

By Rail: Edale station is served daily by frequent trains from Manchester and Sheffield.

By Bus: Service 403, Chesterfield to Edale on summer Sundays and Bank Holidays only.

By Car: Edale is on the minor road which leaves the A625 at Mam Nick and rejoins it at Hope. It is signed at either end.

Refreshments: There are several pubs and cafes in Edale.

Mam Tor

At 1695 feet above sea level, Mam Tor dominates the western end of the Hope Valley and also marks the western terminus of the so-called Great Ridge which runs from its summit eastwards to the summit of Lose Hill.

Its name was probably coined by the Celts and in their language meant "Mother Mountain". It is composed of alternate layers of millstone grit and shales and it is the erosion of the softer shales by weather that has resulted in the impressive landslip on its eastern flank. This geological phenomenon has given rise to an alternative name: "Shivering Mountain".

Its summit is crowned by an Iron Age hill fort extending over 16 acres which makes it the largest in the Peak District. This was probably constructed by the Celts although there is some evidence of Bronze Age occupancy of the site in the form of pottery fragments and charcoal deposits. It would have held a large number of people and even had its own well. The all-round view from there emphasises its strategic position. Although sections of the fort have disappeared with the landslips it is still possible to trace the remains of the defensive ditch.

Edale

Edale was originally a string of small settlements or 'Booths' in the valley bottom. These were the temporary dwellings of forest herdsmen but, with the forest clearances, developed into permanent farmsteads with such names as 'Barber Booth' and 'Nether Booth'. The present church dates from 1886 but this replaced the first, built in 1633. Prior to that date the inhabitants of Edale had to cross the Great Ridge to attend services in Castleton.

Hollins Cross

Hollins Cross marks the spot where coffins were rested on their way from Edale for burial at Castleton. From the name it is obvious that a cross once stood there. Today there are no signs of this but there is a stone cairn erected to the memory of a rambler from Long Eaton.

Chapel Gate

The word 'Gate', used in this sense, means 'Way' and refers to the ancient trackway leading from Edale to Chapel-en-le-Frith.

The Walk

Leave the car park by passing to the left of the toilet block before turning right along the road which passes through the centre of Edale village. Go under the railway bridge and stay forward with the Rambler Inn on your left. By Campion House, turn left onto a path signed to Barber Booth but, almost immediately and in front of the house, go left over a stile. Turn sharp right to reach another stile after 50 yards. Follow the

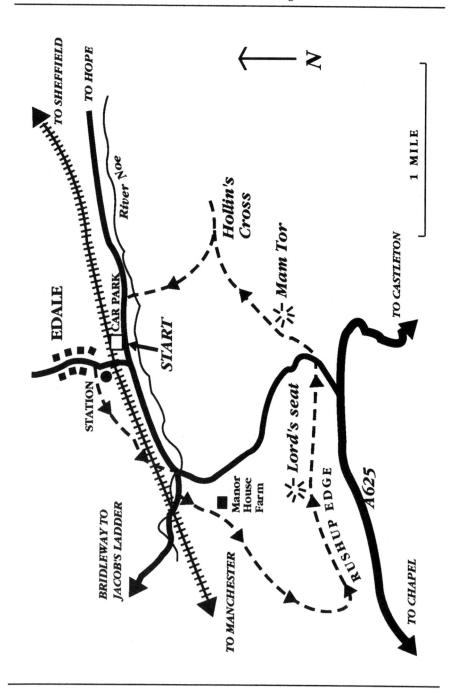

path along the right-hand side of the field and through a gateway, continuing forward with a ditch and a hedge on your right. Rushup Edge is away to the left, Broadlee Bank Tor to the right.

Trig Point, Mam Tor.

Over the next stile, cross the lower end of the field to a stile in the far left-hand corner with the railway running through a cutting on the immediate left. Over the next stile, also in the field corner, advance along a broad track, negotiating a white kissing gate adjacent to a five-barred one before turning left along another track.

After 50 yards cross a stone railway bridge and, on reaching a minor road at Barber Booth, turn right. Within 100 yards this meets the main road through the Edale Valley on a bend. Stay forward over the bridge spanning the River Noe but, at the far end, turn right into a bridleway signed to Upper Booth, Lee House and Hayfield. Initially this has a surface. The River Noe is on the right and its banks are lined with the enormous rhubarb-like leaves of the butterbur. After 200 yards, by a footpath finger post, climb a stile on the left and follow the path with a stream flowing through a deep ditch on your right.

Soon the path crosses the stream by means of a tiny flagstone bridge. On approaching the apparently derelict Manor House Farm turn diagonally right over a stile and advance 50 yards by the side of a boundary fence on your right to another footpath sign and stile. Beyond, the path is clear and easy to follow as it heads for another stile. About 100 yards beyond this, it corners round a breeze block wall. Over the next stile walk to the right of a wall which, ultimately gives way to a fence. Over the next stile there is a fence and a row of hawthorn trees on the right with Rushup Edge directly ahead.

Stay to the right of a wooden stump and to the left of two flat gravestone-type rocks separated by 100 yards before veering right to a stile in a wall after a further 100 yards. Over this turn left to gain another stile after 50 yards. Over this turn right immediately to pass through a five-barred gate before embarking on the long steep climb up the flank of Rushup Edge on a broad track.

In summer this landscape echoes with the call of the curlew while the lapwing perform their stunning aerobatics. It is also the territory of the mountain hare. Originally indigenous to the area, it eventually died out to be re-introduced from Scotland in the 1890s for sporting purposes. It is easier to spot during the winter when its coat turns white.

As you climb you look down into a vast amphitheatre of moorlands rising towards Brown Knoll, with the southern edges of Kinder Scout away to the right across the valley. Reaching a junction of paths with a Peak and Northern Footpath Society sign, go left along the path signed to Chapel-en-le-Frith. From this point the gradient eases and, after about 150 yards, the going levels as the path traverses an extensive moorland plateau where cotton grass waves in the breeze and the golden plover reveals its presence with its eerie piping call.

One solitary landmark is the ventilation shaft from the Cowburn Tunnel. Eventually there opens a view to the south which embraces the Torrs, Coombs Edge, Mount Famine and South Head. At the next footpath junction, recognised by a footpath sign and a stone wall, turn left so that the wall is on your right. The track is clear but stoney until it arrives at the first stile. By the second stile, alongside a five-barred gate, is Lord's Seat, a prehistoric site easily identified by its shape. From there, the track gradually descends through a succession of stiles to reach the minor road which leads from the A625 at Mam Nick into Edale. After negotiating the stile by a five-barred gate, turn right up the road but, after 50 yards, turn left over a broad double stile with a National Trust sign alongside.

Climb the long flight of steps, installed to combat erosion, to the Trig Point on the summit. From there, advance along the Great Ridge along the main path with the village of Castleton nestling below on your right and the often-brooding edges of Kinder away to your left.

The track descends gradually through two stiles to gain Hollins Cross. By the memorial cairn, turn diagonally left but, at the first junction, after 150 yards, fork right following the path signed to Edale. This zig-zags down the slope to a stile. Continue for a further 40 yards to meet a broad track by a footpath sign. Turn left to yet another stile alongside some farm buildings. From that point the route is along the farm approach track. After half a mile a metal five-barred gate is reached with a stile alongside. Turn left to cross a bridge over the River Noe before advancing a further 100 yards to the road.

Turn left for the short distance to the car park.

Great Ridge from Mam Tor.

3. Nine Ladies Stone Circle

After an initial climb this is an easy walk along good clear paths over heather covered heathland.

Route: Stanton-in-the-Peak – Dale View Quarry – The Tower – Nine Ladies Stone Circle – Stanton.

Distance: 3 1/2 miles.

Start: Stanton in the Peak, There is no village car park but it is possible to find parking spaces in the village. Map reference, Church, 241643

Map: "The Peak District, White Peak Area", Number 24 in the Ordnance Survey Outdoor Leisure series.

By Bus: There is a bus service from Matlock and Bakewell Monday to Saturday but no Sunday service.

By Car: Stanton-in-the-Peak is approached by a minor road signed from the centre of Rowsley which is on the A6 south of Bakewell.

Refreshments: Bar meals are available at "The Flying Childers" pub in Stanton. This takes its name from a racehorse.

Nine Ladies Stone Circle

This small stone circle on Stanton Moor is one of several relics left by Stone Age man. It used to be surrounded by a low stone wall but this has now been removed. Today it is almost encircled by birch trees. The name "Nine Ladies" derives from ancient folklore. In pagan times it was customary to dance in circles, a practice frowned upon by the early Church. So, the 'dancers' were turned to stone for perpetuating the rite. Hence the name.

Nine Ladies still has nine stones, the complete ring, although two are leaning at an acute angle. Each stone is between 1 1/2 and 3 feet high and they form a circle about 38 feet in diameter.

Nine Ladies, Stanton Moor.

There are indications of an encircling bank with two gaps, obviously for entrances. In the centre is a small mound which may have been higher before nineteenth century excavations. About 130 feet away in a West-South-Westerly direction, is another upright stone, a 3-foot high slab known as "The King's Stone".

The Tower

The square gritstone tower overlooking the lower Derwent Valley was erected in 1832 by Lieutenant Colonel William Thornhill of Stanton Hall to mark the successful passage of the 1832 Reform Act.

The Walk

From the centre of the village of Stanton-in-the-Peak walk up School Lane which is signed to Birchover. After a quarter of a mile, fork left into a minor road signed to Stanton Lees. Climb to the top of the hill. Ignore the first footpath sign on the right indicating a path to Nine Ladies. Stay with the narrow road as it descends to pass Dale View quarry which is on your left.

A few yards beyond the quarry entrance turn right over a step stile which is graced by a faded footpath sign. Cross the field to a facing wood, staying some 20 yards to the left of the field boundary and a row of stately oak trees. Over the stile, enter the deciduous woods. Immediately fork right in front of a facing wall. At the top of a small embankment turn right at a T-junction and continue climbing to reach a wall on your right.

Stay to the left of the wall through the edge of the wood, with open fields and a television mast visible on the right. As the woods eventually close in the gradient levels out and the path quickly acquires a fence on the right.

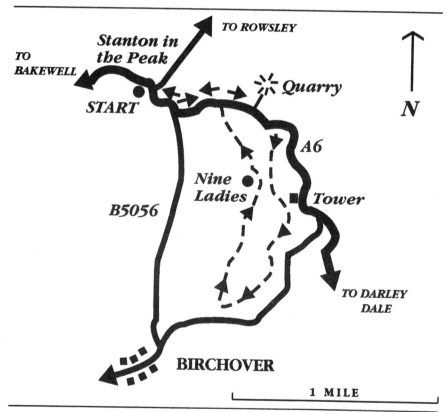

At the next T-junction turn left but, on gaining a Y-junction close to the Tower and recognisable by a National Trust sign, fork left. The terrain is heathland, rather more reminiscent of Dorset than Derbyshire. There is also a fine view down into the southern section of the Derwent Valley.

When a large rock with "EIN 1831" carved onto it is reached, turn sharp right. Within 50 yards another T-junction is met. Go left. There is now a good, firm and wide path crossing heather-covered heathland which also has bracken. Stay to the left of a fence until, eventually, the path swings round to the right. By the next National Trust sign, adjacent to another large rock, turn right over a stile but then fork left towards a ruined building. At the T-junction turn right to gain a cross roads in the path system within a further 250 yards.

Continue forwards along the path, now signed to Nine Ladies. After some distance the stone circle appears to the left of the path, almost encircled by birch trees.

After your visit return to the path to continue along it to a stile by a five-barred gate. Maintain direction, negotiate a squeezer stile, cross a field, pass through a gateway and advance to another squeezer stile by the road. Turn left down the hill into Stanton.

4. Carl Wark

A moderate route on good moorland tracks and paths. There are some fine moorland views.

Route: Car park – Burbage Bridge – Burbage Rocks – Upper Burbage Bridge – Higger Tor – Carl Wark – Over Owler Tor – Car park.

Distance: 5 1/2 miles

Start: Car park on the A625 between Millstone Edge and the "Fox House" Inn. Map Reference 251801

Map: Sheet 743, SK28/38, "Sheffield", in the Ordnance Survey's "Pathfinder" series.

By Bus: There is a bus service from Sheffield to Castleton.

By Car: The starting point is on the A625 between Hathersage and the "Fox House" Inn.

Refreshment: None on the route. There is a selection of cafes and pubs serving food in Hathersage. The "Fox House" Inn also serves bar food.

Carl Wark Hill Fort

Controversy surrounds the date of Carl Wark hill fort, which is to be found near Burbage Brook above Hathersage. It is generally thought to be from the Iron Age period but some authorities dispute this, claiming that it is of much later origin. The truth of the matter appears to be that it was fortified during the Ice Age with sophistications added at a later date, perhaps as late as the Saxon period. It was built on a rocky knoll and consists of a huge platform of gritstone blocks measuring as much as five feet across. This is surrounded by ramparts ten feet high.

On the northern, more vulnerable side, an earthen bank was constructed and a drystone wall built. The entrance was at the southern end where there was also a guard room. As with most Iron Age hillforts, it may have contained buildings inside and also served as an administrative and religious centre.

Carl Wark

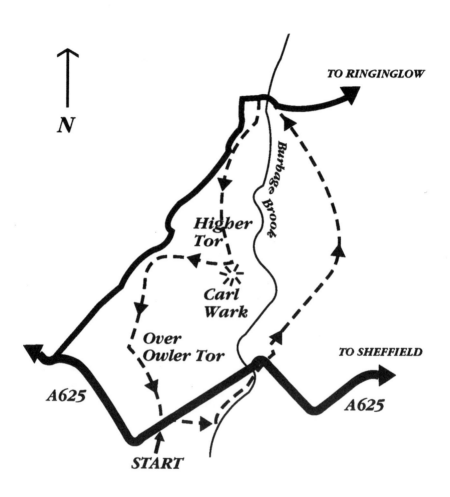

TO RINGINGLOW

N

Burbage Brook

Higher
Tor

Carl
Wark

Over
Owler Tor

TO SHEFFIELD

A625

A625

START

1 MILE

Climbing on Burbage Rocks

The Walk

Leaving the car, park turn left along the A625. After 50 yards, and by two stone gateposts, veer right along a clear path which descends the bracken-covered slope to a wooden kissing gate within ten yards. Continue for a further 100 yards to a Y-junction. Fork left to arrive at a footbridge spanning Burbage Brook. Do not cross. Instead, turn left to follow the brook upstream.

By the next footbridge, veer left to a small gate before making an exit onto the A625 by a Derbyshire boundary sign. Turn right. Cross Burbage Bridge and then turn left up a flight of eleven steps to a stile. Advance forward 100 yards to a junction with a broad track. Turn left. Stay with this track as Carl Wark becomes visible ahead.

Do not fork either to the right or left in crossing this vast saucer of moorland encompassed by gritstone edges which are topped occasionally by crags and other strangely fashioned rock formations. By a waymarker post continue forward along the main track which curves round to the left to a second waymarker post within 30 yards. Ignore a very clear path heading off to the right. Stay with the main track.

Accompanied by wheatear, meadow pippit, cuckoo and skylark in summer, pass beneath Burbage Rocks, a favourite haunt of climbers to reach a wooden gate by Upper Burbage Bridge.

Turn left along the road. At the far end of the second bridge turn left. Within a few yards negotiate the stile on the left and then fork right immediately onto a path which runs above the rocks. Burbage Brook is now in the valley to the left.

The path clings to the contour before climbing to the summit of Higger

Higger Tor

Tor. This may simply be a corruption of Higher Tor or it may refer to some long-forgotten pagan god. A T-junction is reached on the summit. Turn left to enjoy the wide ranging views of the White Peak, Stanage Moors and Hope Valley.

Keep to the eastern edge of the summit plateau to a point opposite where you came up and then follow the path which wends its way down through the rocks before heading across the open moors to Carl Wark.

Just before the final ascent of Carl Wark turn onto the path which runs round the western side of the base. This tends to swing to the right before meeting a T-junction. Turn right there, onto a narrower but distinct path which climbs gently through the heather to meet a cross-roads in the path network at Wynyard's Nick, another excellent viewpoint.

Turn left onto the path which climbs over Over Owler Tor before descending the gradual slope to the car park at the starting point.

Over Owler Tor

Upper Burbage Bridge.

5. The Roman Fort at Navio

This is mainly a moorland walk involving some long climbs followed by a steep descent. The final section follows field paths.

Route: Hope – Hope Cross – Winhill Pike – Aston – Brough – Navio – Hope.

Distance: 9 miles.

Start: Car park Hope. Map Reference 172835

Map: "The Peak District, Dark Peak Area", Number 1 in the Ordnance Survey's Outdoor Leisure series.

By Bus: There are daily buses from Sheffield, Chesterfield Castleton. Other buses run from Bakewell from Monday to Friday, from Buxton on Tuesdays, Thursdays and Saturdays and from Hanley on Saturdays and Sundays. Buses operate from Barnsley, Mansfield, Stockport, Ilkeston and Staveley on summer Sundays and Bank Holidays.

By Train: There is a frequent daily service to Hope from Manchester and Sheffield.

By Car: Hope is on the A625 road.

Refreshments: There are several cafes and pubs in Hope village.

Navio

Today there is little evidence of the Roman fort at Navio except for a slight rise in a field just to the west of the present-day village of Brough. Standing on the site, it is very easy to appreciate its strategic position with views along the Hope Valley and of the Great Ridge, Winhill Pike and the White Peak.

Obviously constructed to safeguard the lead mining interests of the Romans in the Peak District, it was the only fort within the boundaries of the present National Park. It was the focal point of the road network with routes fanning out to Templeborough, near Rotherham, Melandra, the Roman fort near Glossop, and to Buxton which, even then, was an important spa town.

Sections of these Roman roads may still be seen. There is one paved stretch now known as Doctor's Gate along the southern fringe of Bleaklow while the one to Buxton, Batham Gate, traverses Bradwell Moor. One length of the road to Melandra is used in this route. The fort, covering about two acres, probably housed a garrison of 500 men.

Hope Cross

This square stone guide post dates back to the days when the tracks which converge there were the main trans-Pennine highways for the Jaggers with their trains of packhorses. Its square top bears the legends "Glossop", "Sheffield", "Edale" and "Hope".

Win Hill Pike

Win Hill is associated with Lose Hill which faces it across the Noe valley. Tradition has it that there was a battle nearby between the armies of Northumbria and Wessex. The victors camped on Win Hill, the losers on Lose Hill.

The fighting, so it is said, was so bitter that the river flowed red with blood. The Northumbrians were driven back up Win Hill but eventually turned the tables on their attackers by rolling large boulders down the slopes.

In January, 1764, a grazier and his servant, on their way to Ireland, perished in a blizzard on Win Hill. Their bodies were not discovered until the snow thawed in May. Because they "smelt so strong" they were buried where they were found. 20 years later, when they were exhumed for re-burial, their bodies were found to be in a state of perfect preservation.

Statuette above the entrance to Hope Church

The Walk

From the car park begin by turning right along the A625 but, after about 100 yards, and opposite Hope Church, make a left turn into Edale Road.

With a quarter of a mile behind you, and opposite a house called "Kilncroft", fork right into a minor road signed as a cul-de-sac. Cross Killhill Bridge, a stone structure over the River Noe, before continuing along the surfaced road to pass another house christened "Mill Barn".

Pass beneath the railway to a Y-junction. Fork left, ignoring the signed path to the right. By the entrance to "The Homestead" fork left again this time into an unsurfaced lane. Pass to the right of "The Coach House" to a squeezer stile before following the field path as it keeps to the left of a wall.

Aim for the gateway ahead, then stay to the left of a fence until Fullwood Stile farm is reached. Turn right over a stile by a five-barred gate, turn left onto a track which stays to the left of the farm but turn right by the corner of the barn.

After 5 yards, by the farm entrance, turn left to meet a bridleway on a bend. Stay forward. From this point the long gradual climb along the bridleway begins. In summer it is lined with meadow cranesbill, ragged robin, ragwort, foxglove, and red campion.

Pass through a five-barred gate, still climbing, until the trains heading for Edale resemble toys. The gradient eases as the track runs along the contour for half a mile with superb views up Edale and of the northern aspect of the Great Ridge from Lose Hill to Mam Tor. The bridleway passes through one more five-barred gate before reaching Hope Cross, having followed the line of the Roman road which linked Navio with Melandra, near Glossop.

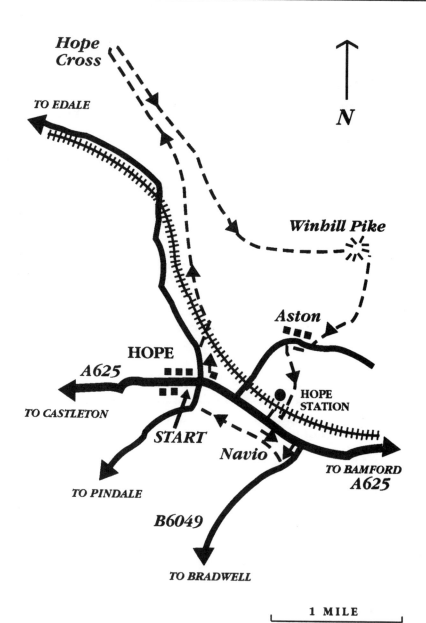

Roman Road from Hope Cross

At this spot we leave the Roman road. Proceed just a few yards beyond Hope Cross, pass through another five-barred gate, turn sharp right for 20 yards, turn right again over a stile and proceed forward with a conifer plantation on the left and a wall on your right.

Initially you are walking parallel to the outward route but, after 250 yards, veer leftwards. Beyond the next stile continue in the same direction but now with a broken stone wall on your left. The fine clear path climbs gradually. Where the conifer plantation swings away to the left continue forward onto the heather-covered moors which encircle Win Hill Pike.

After some considerable distance of easy climbing the path swings eastwards and levels at it meets a wall on your right. This wall terminates after 400 yards but stay with the distinct path to a finger post where two paths intersect each other. Keep forward for the final climb to the rugged, rocky summit of Win Hill Pike. From there you can enjoy a magnificent panorama embracing the Derwent Edges, Ladybower Reservoir, the Hope Valley, Bamford Edge, the Bradwell valley and both Bretton and Eyam Edges. It is one of the finest viewpoints in the Peak District.

Trig point, Win Hill Pike

The path stays a few feet to the right of the Trig Point before dropping rapidly to a double stile. At the Y-junction beyond fork left towards a plantation. Enter the trees to reach a fence-cum-wall with a stile. Do not climb over. Instead, turn right along a broad path which keeps to the contour but careful navigation is required.

By the third stone wall running off to your right, and ten yards beyond an oblong stone trough, also on the right, fork right by a wall corner to pass through a wall gap. Immediately beyond, turn left. Almost at once the path veers right to climb the slope through the heather but soon descends steeply between two banks to a ladder stile. Continue in the same direction to the far right-hand corner of the field and, over the stile there, continue with a row of trees on your left and a drystone wall on your right. As the field widens, stay to the left-hand side of the field. This is not difficult because the path is well used. Soon a stile provides access to a lane which, after 50 yards, exits onto the Aston to Thornhill road.

Turn right to walk through Aston village, passing the substantial Jacobean manor house on your right. At the road junction, continue

Turn right, and where this road forms a junction with the Pindale one, make another turn to the right to walk the short distance back into Hope village and the car park.

6. Roystone Grange

This is an easy walk mainly along trails, bridleways and field paths.

Route: Minninglow car park – High Peak Trail – Roystone Grange – Gallowlow Lane – Gotham Plantation – Minninglow car park.

Distance: 5 miles

Start: Minninglow car park, $3/4$ mile south of the hamlet of Pikehall which is on the A5012 Newhaven to Cromford road. Map Reference 195582

Map: "The Peak District, White Peak Area", number 24 in Ordnance Survey's Outdoor Leisure series.

By Bus: No services to Pikehall.

By Car: Minninglow car park, adjacent to the High Peak Trail, is signed from the A5012 Newhaven to Cromford road in the centre of Pikehall.

Refreshments: None on the route.

Roystone Grange

A few years ago David Twigge, the then owner of Roystone Grange Farm near Ballidon, decided to enlarge his dairy. On digging the foundations he unearthed a woman's body. Coincidentally Richard Hodges, a Lecturer in Archaeology at Sheffield University, was nearby with a party of students. They examined the burial which turned out to be the remains of a woman of the Roman period interred by the side of a pond. This led Richard Hodges and a team of archaeologists to examine the valley in detail. Not only did they unearth a Roman farm but also the foundations of a medieval monastic grange.

In view of the fact that the surrounding area is rich in tumuli such as the burial mound on Minninglow, which overlooks the farm, they suspect that this secluded dry valley may have a history of human occupation dating back about 6,000 years.

On the wall of the present dairy, the Peak District National Park has fixed an interpretive board showing the remains of the Roman period. The centre-piece was a manor house measuring some 20 metres long by 12 metres wide. It would have had rubble walls supporting a thatched roof. Scattered on the surrounding hillsides the remains of smaller farms have been discovered.

According to Ken Smith, the National Park's Archaeologist, no Romans ever lived at Roystone. The occupants were hill farmers of local stock and so the building had no traces of mosaics. The manor had its own farmyard, surrounded by drystone walls, remnants of which still survive, having been incorporated into later structures. About 400 yards to the south, the remains of the Roman field system may still be seen.

The Medieval Grange

The medieval grange at Roystone dates from the reign of King Henry II when the valley passed into the ownership of the Cistercian Abbey of Garendon in Leicestershire. Worked by a team of lay brothers it became

Exavations at Roystone Grange, 1992

a ranch until, following the plagues of the fourteenth century and a deterioration in the weather, it was leased to a tenant farmer.

Two of the monastic buildings have been excavated in recent years and the foundations have been left partially exposed for inspection by visitors. The remaining rubble and stone foundations of the dairy show it to have been 17 metres long by 12 wide. In the central room was a hearth for warming milk and, at one end of the parlour, was an oven. Animal bones discovered on the medieval site prove that sheep were the principal livestock but cattle, pigs and even geese were eaten on occasion. Work on the Roman site continues. In the summer of 1992, a team from Sheffield found a Romano-British hearth which will encourage further excavations in the years ahead.

The present large stone building close by the medieval grange was a nineteenth century pump house. A water-cooled engine pumped compressed air through cast-iron pipes to drive the drills used in the various quarries which the walker may still see along the High Peak Trail.

The Walk

Leaving the car park, head eastwards along the High Peak Trail in the signed direction of Middleton Top and High Peak Junction. Immediately out of the car park, cross a narrow road and continue along the Trail with Minninglow in the distance and a farm nestling in the valley below to the right.

As the Trail curves round in a large bend to the right glance backwards to glimpse the splendid drystone walling which supports the embankment. It is incredible to contemplate that this extensive and well crafted stonework was all done by hand. As Minninglow is approached it is clear that it is crowned with spindly-looking Scots Pines.

The Trail itself is lined with a profusion of wild flowers including harebells, clover, scabious, ox-eye daisy, saxifrage, knapweed, thistles and birdsfoot trefoil. Larger species to be found are elder, bramble and even heather.

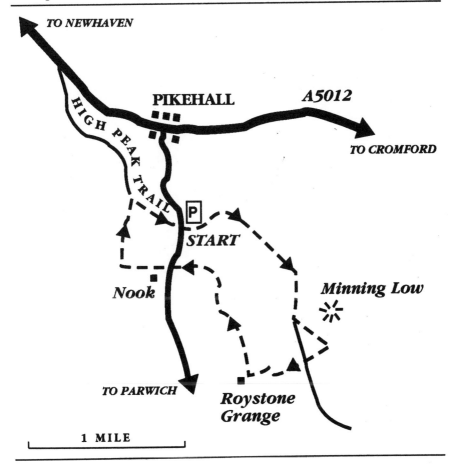

After passing through a limestone cutting, the route passes a disused quarry littered with abandoned machinery, a kind of living museum. A quarter of a mile further and there is another unusual industrial relic. This is a stone-built brick kiln on the left. It was obviously a precursor of the more modern brickworks at nearby Friden.

Eventually two five-barred gates, separated by a few yards, are reached. Pass through the first, and fork left over a stile adjacent to yet another five-barred gate onto a wide, walled and green lane. After a further quarter of a mile, and just before the lane begins a short climb, turn right over a waymarked stile, head directly for a stone bridge carrying the High Peak Trail and proceed through another five-barred gate.

Minninglow and the High Peak Trail.

The path, broad and clear, crosses a field dropping towards the valley as it negotiates a squeezer stile. Continue the descent to a stone step stile in the wall on the left, before making a right turn to pass through a gateway. Stay close to the wall on your left for 100 yards. Turn through another stile and cross a small field diagonally to a stone step stile which affords access onto a wide track. Turn left to examine the nineteenth century pump house and the remains of the medieval grange.

Turn round and retrace your steps along the track to the present farmhouse where you will see the Roman remains. Look out for a magnificent peacock as you pass the farm, and stay with the track as it climbs gradually up the valley.

Five yards after the third five-barred gate, a T-junction is reached. Turn left into Gallowlow Lane, climbing gradually for a quarter of a mile to the junction with a road. Cross directly into another lane initially running alongside Cobblersnook Plantation which is on your right. Just beyond, pass "The Nook", a small white cottage on your left.

Today's farmhouse at Roystone Grange.

Stay with the lane until reaching a footpath finger post. Turn right over the stile, and cross directly across the centre of the field to another stile approximately 15 yards to the left of a gap in the facing wall. Maintain direction across the second field to a stile by the corner of a plantation. From there, veer sharply to the right, cross a field and reach a stile about 100 yards to the right of the plantation.

Stay forward for ten yards over a muddy patch in the gap between the trees to a stile adjacent to a five-barred gate. Maintain direction, with a wall on the right and pass to the left of a strangely-shaped water trough to reach a bent gatepost. It is the most unusual one I have ever seen.

Corner right by this, staying close to the wall on your right, to a stile set in the right-hand corner of the field. Over that turn right along the High Peak Trail but, before continuing, look leftwards at how the trail curves. It is said to have been the tightest bend on any railway in this country.

It is approximately a quarter of a mile eastwards along the Trail to Minninglow car park, a former goods yard on the Cromford and High Peak Railway.

High Peak Trail, Roystone.

7. Peveril Castle, Castleton

A moderate walk involving one long and several short but steep climbs, followed by a steep descent and a riverside walk.

Route: Castleton – Hollins Cross – Back Tor – Lose Hill – Hope – Castleton.

Distance: $6\,^1/_4$ miles.

Start: Car Park, Castleton. Map Reference 149830.

Map: "The Peak District, Dark Peak Area", Number 1 in the Ordnance Survey's Outdoor Leisure Series.

By Rail: The nearest railway station is Hope, a little over $1^1/_2$ miles from the start. It is served by frequent trains from Manchester and Sheffield.

By Bus: Daily services from Sheffield and Chesterfield. On summer Sundays and Bank Holidays, there are buses from Buxton, Barnsley, Huddersfield, Glossop and Leek.

By Car: The car park is signed in the centre of Castleton on the A625, Whaley Bridge to Sheffield road.

Refreshments: There are several cafes and pubs in both Castleton and Hope.

Peveril Castle

Peveril Castle is so situated high above the village of Castleton, that it requires a separate visit to be made. The views from the keep however, provide ample reward whether the visit is made either before or after this walk. They embrace the village itself, nestling at the foot of the slope, plus the entire length of the Great Ridge from Mam Tor to Lose Hill.

The village itself was originally planned and encircled by a ditch, so that the inhabitants could receive protection from the garrison stationed within the castle. This was established shortly after the Conquest of 1066 by William Peveril, one of William's most trusted knights who had accompanied him from France. He had been given several manors in the Peak, which was regarded as a buffer zone between the Midlands and the wilder, more rebellious North. The castle was also important in guarding the Crown's interests in the lead mining interest in the vicinity.

Work must have commenced quickly, because Peveril Castle is mentioned in the Domesday Book of 1086. The first section to be constructed was probably the north wall, because this was the site's most vulnerable side.

Peveril Castle

On Peveril's death in 1114, the castle was inherited by his son, another William, but he fell foul of King Henry II, and was made to forfeit the castle to the Crown. Henry paid several visits to Castleton, and it was in the castle that he received the submission of King Malcolm IV of Scotland in 1157.

He was one of the greatest of castle builders, so it is not surprising that he made additions to the Castle of the Peak, as it was then known. These additions included the keep, (erected in 1177 at a cost of £200), the old hall and the gatehouse. The only occasion on which Peveril Castle was involved in real military action was in the year following Runnymede, when there was a rebellion of some of the barons against King John.

Later kings maintained the castle in good repair and several made visits. At one date, a new hall was added, but shortly after 1369, King Edward III granted it to his son, John of Gaunt, and so Peveril passed under the control of the Duchy of Lancaster. By 1480, we learn that the castle had "become much decayed", and by 1561, although the keep was used as a courthouse, the bailey served as a pound for stray sheep.

In the seventeenth century, the Duchy of Lancaster paid for repairs to the remains, then very much as we see them today. In 1932, the castle passed to the Ministry of Works, now English Heritage.

The Walk

Leave the car park by the ginnel or path in the corner opposite the toilet block. At the far end, after a few yards, make a left turn into Hollowford Lane. Before the Training Centre, fork left and, at the subsequent junction, fork left again.

Pass a field barn on your right and negotiate a stile adjacent to a five-barred gate. 200 yards beyond, where the lane bends left and by a judiciously placed seat, stay forward over a stile and onto a path which climbs gradually between hawthorn trees.

At the next gate go left over a stile with a path signed to Hollins Cross. Continue climbing steeply up the bracken-covered slope, negotiating a couple of stiles before reaching the stepped section. Once again this has been made necessary to combat erosion.

The crest of the ridge is reached at Hollins Cross. Pause awhile to admire the all-round view which embraces both the Dark and White Peaks. Turn right to follow the well-trodden path which stays along the crest of the Great Ridge, passing a redundant stile plus one still in use. At the next junction, at the bottom of a dip, turn left over a stile, and

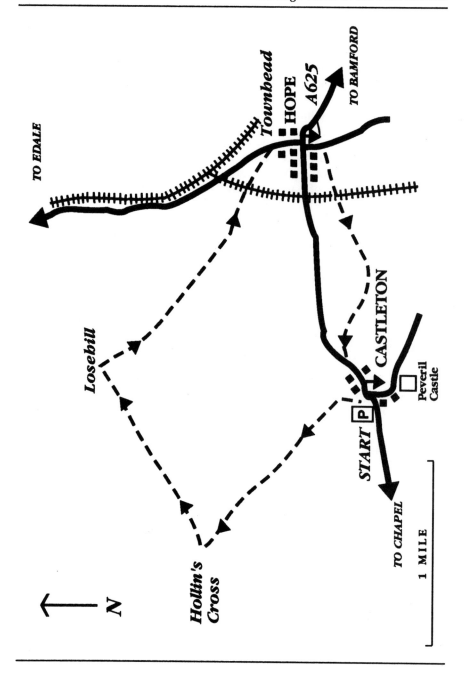

immediately turn right for the steepish climb to the summit of Back Tor. From there, maintain the line of direction to the left of a wire fence with Lose Hill looming ahead.

Hollins Cross

After levelling for a while, the path resumes its uphill course to a stile from where a line of stone cairns guide the walker to the summit of Lose Hill at 1563 feet. The land around the summit is known as "Ward's Piece" dedicated to the memory of G. H. B. Ward, one of the early campaigners for open access.

From the summit continue with the path as it swings right for a steep descent to a double stile. Ignore a path to the left. Advance a further 100 yards to a T-junction. Turn left. There is now a broken wall on your right and the path is still losing height.

From the next footpath sign, follow the direction of Hope, passing behind Losehill Farm to a gateway and another footpath sign. Again choose the direction of Hope, ignoring a stile on the right and following a field path to the left of a wall. Beyond the next stile there is a

T-junction. Go right, now with a wider track, to yet another stile. This provides access to a sunken lane. Follow this, using two more stiles, until it meets the Edale to Hope road at Townhead. Turn right along the road to meet the A625 in the centre of Hope village.

Opposite the church, turn right along the A625. After about 20 yards, turn left into Pindale road so that the church is now on your left. Cross the stone bridge and pass the entrance to Eccles Lane on your left before reaching a footpath sign on the right indicating a footpath to Castleton. Turn right over the stile, head for another stile and then turn right by the field boundary with a river on your right.

Proceed over more stiles, cross the branch railway line leading to Hope Cement Works and negotiate a succession of stiles across more fields until the path runs along the river bank to pass the sewage works. After one more stile the path becomes a walled lane until it reaches the A625 in Castleton. Turn left along the road for the village centre and car park.

Note: Castleton has several other attractions apart from Peveril Castle. These include several show caves, all advertised in the village, and nearby Odin's Mine.

8. Pilsbury Castle

A gentle walk through lush countryside on field paths.

Route: Hartington – Carder Low – Pilsbury Castle – Pilsbury – Harris Close Farm – Hartington.

Distance: 5 $^1/_2$ miles.

Start: Hartington village square. Map Reference 128604

Map: "The Peak District, White Peak Area", Number 24 in Ordnance Survey's Outdoor Leisure series.

By Bus: Daily service, except Sundays, from Buxton and Ashbourne. Buses on summer Sundays and Bank Holidays from Newcastle, Congleton, Macclesfield, Coal Aston, Bakewell, Mansfield, Derby and Barnsley. Buses from Leek on Wednesdays only. Walkers from Manchester and Stockport will need to change in Buxton.

By Car: Hartington is situated on the B5054. It is signed from the A 515 Buxton to Newhaven road.

Refreshments: There are several pubs and cafes in Hartington.

Pilsbury Castle

Pilsbury Castle probably dates from the same period as Peveril Castle at Castleton, but it never achieved the same status. It was built by William the Conqueror to subdue the local tribes and was a Motte and Bailey Castle.

Because the original wooden structure was never replaced by stone, there is nothing to see today except the strangely-shaped rock on which it was built. Even so, it is still possible to appreciate why this particular spot was chosen. It would have been very hard to attack and it was ideally placed for keeping a watching brief on the upper valleys of both the Dove and Manifold.

Pilsbury Castle

By the fourteenth century, the castle had ceased to be occupied. It is possible to walk round the site on a concessionary footpath. The National Park has erected an explanatory panel.

The Upper Dove

For those walkers anxious to avoid the crowds which throng that section of Dovedale between Hartington and Thorpe Upper Dovedale is ideal. It is much quieter and although the scenery is perhaps less dramatic it is, nonetheless, very attractive with some fine views of Chrome Hill on the outward leg of this walk.

Hartington

Hartington is one of the most popular tourist venues in the Peak District. With its mellow stone houses and shops clustered round the mere it realises the imaginary, idealised picture of what a country village ought to look like. Historically it was far more important than it is now.

It enjoyed the privilege of holding the first market in the Peak District, thanks to a charter granted as early as 1203. The market is no longer held.

It acquired a Town Hall in 1836 but much earlier, in the seventeenth century, it was associated with Izaak Walton, the author of "The Compleat Angler" who often stayed at Beresford Hall, a mile south of Hartington, with his friend Charles Cotton who built a Fishing House near the Dove. It is not possible to visit this but from the riverside path it just possible to catch a glimpse. Hartington is also renowned for its Blue Stilton cheese which is still manufactured in the dairy close to the centre along with Buxton Blue, Dovedale and other brands. All are on sale in the Cheese Shop by the mere.

The Walk

Leave Hartington village centre along the B5054 which is signed to Ashbourne. After 50 yards, and opposite a telephone kiosk, turn left into a minor road which climbs gradually to pass the church on your right and, subsequently, a substantial house, "Grey Gables".

Ignore a signed path to the left just beyond. Instead continue up the slope to the point where the road bends to the right. Turn left over a stile with a footpath sign adjacent and head for the waymarked step stile some 15 yards to the left of a gateway. Veer diagonally left to another stile and then right, crossing the centre of a field to a stile. Over that, turn left immediately and, staying to the right of a wall, head for a waymarked gateway to join a farm track.

Turn left and advance 100 yards before turning right through a waymarked five-barred gate. Turn slightly to the right on a broad green path which runs just to the left of a wall, traversing a grassy terrace above the valley of the River Dove with Chrome Hill conspicuous in the far distance. The slope is scattered with rocks. After some distance negotiate a stile and maintain line of direction to a second before climbing gently over the shoulder of Carder Low. After a slight drop, continue ahead along the contour to a stile which has a very large limestone block as a mounting step, one of the most unusual I have ever seen.

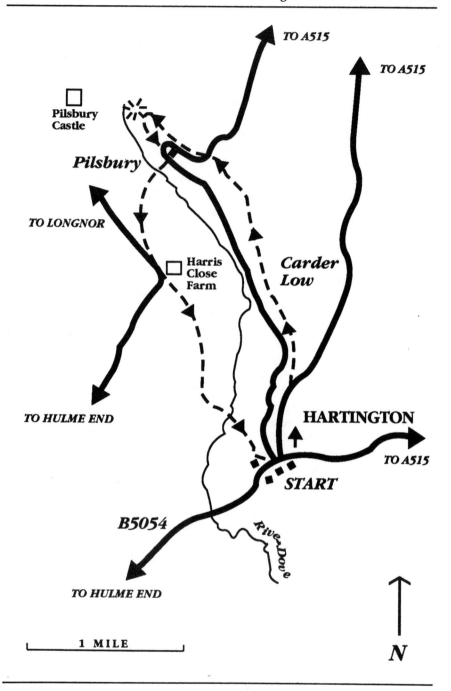

TO A515

TO A515

Pilsbury
Castle

Pilsbury

TO LONGNOR

Harris
Close
Farm

*Carder
Low*

TO HULME END

HARTINGTON

TO A515

START

B5054

River Dove

TO HULME END

1 MILE

N

Immediately over, at a junction, fork right to a waymarked five-barred gate and then stay to the left of a derelict farm to reach another wooden five-barred gate.

Follow the farm track as it veers away to the left to reach a stile alongside a gate. Over that, veer right away from the track, crossing more pasture land to a squeezer stile which permits access to a road. Cross directly to a stile and a path signed to Crowdecote and Longnor. Traverse the first field to an obvious stile before going to the right but keeping close to a wall on your left to reach a stone step stile after 50 yards.

Over that, stay to the left of a wall along a broad, grassy path with Pilsbury hamlet down below on the left. At the subsequent Y-junction fork left, soon passing a wall-end and rounding a small hillock to a footpath sign. There, veer left down the slope to meet a bridleway by Pilsbury Castle and the National Park's explanatory panel. On reaching the junction with the bridleway, turn left to reach the tiny hamlet of Pilsbury after a quarter of a mile. Turn right along the gated road which is signed to Hartington with a large imposing house set back a little on your left-hand side.

Through the first gate, turn right along a broad meadow path to a footbridge over the infant Dove. At the far end turn right as waymarked. Climb to a footpath finger post. There turn left over a stile for the long gradual climb along a path signposted to Sheen. After 100 yards, fork left up the slope eventually gaining a waymarked stile.

Beyond, head for a wall on the right, at a distance of about 20 yards, before veering left to stay alongside it. After 90 yards, turn right through a squeezer stile before heading diagonally left through a gateway as you aim for a distant clump of trees on the crest of the hill. As you approach it will become obvious that these form a shelter belt to what is now a small, unoccupied house with a barn attached.

Stay to the left of the trees to a stile. Then, with the house on your right, cross the field to a wooden stile set into a wire fence against a hawthorn hedge. Over that, immediately turn right through a five-barred gate to the road from Sheen to Longnor. From here there is a fine view of Sheen Hill with its rocky summit.

Turn left along the road for 250 yards. By Harris Close Farm, dated 1847, turn left into the drive, However, almost immediately turn right to pass the right-hand corner of an outbuilding which displays a white sign reading "FOOTPATH".

Walk between the buildings and a wall on your right to a squeezer stile. From there stay to the left of a wall, the line of the path being easy to follow as it runs through a series of stiles to a conifer plantation. Stay just inside the boundary wall of the plantation but being careful to avoid low branches and slippery roots. Leave the plantation by a step stile but still maintain the same line of direction, staying just to the left of the wall, until reaching a T-junction.

Leave the field by a stile in the wall on your right and turn left along what is initially a sunken lane. After emerging from two flanking low banks into the open maintain your line down the grassy slope to a stile in a wire fence. Cross directly over a lane to another stile before proceeding down the field to a stone footbridge. At the far end, turn sharp right to pass through a succession of obvious stiles until emerging onto the narrow road by the entrance to Nuttall's Dairy. Turn left along this road for the very short distance to your starting point in the centre of Hartington.

9. Lyme Hall

A mainly moorland route following good tracks and paths while offering some superb views of both Macclesfield Forest and the western fringes of Kinder Scout.

Route: Lyme Hall – Green Close – Pott Shrigley – Bowstones – Lantern Wood – Lyme Hall

Distance: 8 1/2 miles

Start: Car park, Lyme Park. Map Reference 964824

Maps: 1) "Stockport (South)". Number 741 in the Ordnance Survey's Pathfinder series; 2) "The Peak District, White Peak Area", Number 24 in the Ordnance Survey's Outdoor Leisure series.

By Train: There is a half hourly service from Manchester Piccadilly and Buxton to Disley station which is about 1¹/₂ miles from Lyme car park.

By Bus: Trent bus services 198 and 199, Buxton to Stockport, and Greater Manchester Buses route 361 Glossop to Stockport, stop at the main gate of Lyme, one mile from the car park. Starline service number 3, Macclesfield to Kettleshulme, and Trent service X67, Nottingham to Manchester, (Trans Peak), both stop at the Ram's Head in Disley, 1¹/₂ miles from the start of the walk.

By Car: Lyme Park is signed from the A6 trunk between High Lane and Disley. Admission to the park for a car is £3, including occupants, and £2 for a motor cycle (in 1993)

Refreshments: The Tea Room in Lyme Hall serves light meals, snacks and beverages. The Kiosk in the car park sells soft drinks, tea, coffee and confectionery. Both are open daily between Easter and early October from 11.00 to 17.30 hours.

Lyme Hall

Lyme Park, or Lyme Handley as it is officially known, was originally a

Lyme Hall

part of the Royal Forest of Macclesfield, established after the Norman Conquest of 1066.

In 1346, King Edward III granted it to Thomas Danyers as a reward for the courage he had shown alongside the Black Prince during the campaigns in France. In 1388, Peter Legh married Margaret, daughter of Danyers, and nine years later Lyme passed into his possession. His descendants lived at Lyme until 1946 when the property and park were given to the National Trust. At the outset, the residence was little more than a wooden hunting lodge but, after 1465, it became a much more substantial building.

In 1570, a later Peter Legh decided to extend the house by adding what now forms the East and West sides, but much of the present shape was determined by the Italian architect, Giacomo Leoni who designed its outstanding classical appearance by creating the famous South Front and courtyard, as well as completing the West Front. Later additions were made in the nineteenth century. Today's visitor may see the interior including the Entrance Hall, Chapel, Grand Staircase, Saloon, and Long Gallery as well as various bedrooms. The Knight's Room is said to be haunted. Certainly during one set of alterations a skeleton, believed to be that of a priest, was discovered under the floorboards. The Leghs were staunch supporters of the Royalist cause during the Civil War of the seventeenth century, so afterwards the Duke of York, later to become King James II, stayed at Lyme. After his flight in 1688, meetings were held in the Hall to plot his restoration.

From its earliest days, Lyme has been a deer park, famous for its red stags. The herd was formed from those in Macclesfield Forest. Fallow deer were introduced in medieval times and, along with the red, provided both sport and meat. Royalty, including James II, hunted there. The red deer still roam freely but the fallow died out during the early years of this century. However, they were re-introduced in 1980 and have their own large sanctuary within the park.

Although there is no definite proof, it is believed that Mary, Queen of Scots, stayed at Lyme while she was a prisoner of Queen Elizabeth I and staying in Buxton.

Lyme Cage, which is a landmark for miles around, was erected on Cage Hill in 1524 as an observation tower for ladies and other guests to watch the hunting. In later times it was used as a lock-up for poachers and, until 1970, served as the house of the Park Keeper.

Lyme, although it belongs to the National Trust, is administered by Stockport Metropolitan Borough Council. It has been designated as a Country Park and recently opened a Countryside Centre to explain the natural history to be found there. The car park is also the official northern starting point for the Gritstone Trail, an 18-mile walking trail established by Cheshire County Council. It runs to Rushton Spencer on the Staffordshire boundary where it links in with the Staffordshire Way. There are also many waymarked walking routes in and around the park. A circuit of the boundary walls is 9 miles in length.

Bowstones

The Bowstones, which are to be found near the farm of the same name above Lyme are considered to be of Saxon origin, possibly the bases of two crosses, the shafts of which are still preserved at Lyme Hall. Apart from having some religious significance, they may have served as boundary markers or landmarks for the ridings of Macclesfield Forest or even of some long-forgotten Saxon kingdom.

The Bowstones

The Walk

Keeping well to the right of the children's playground, head across to the south west corner of the car park and a wooden finger post which signals the start of the Gritstone Trail, a medium length route which runs to Rushton Spencer.

Veer left by the sign and, after 15 yards, negotiate a large wooden kissing gate. Follow the wide rough track as it climbs gradually with a tall drystone wall on your left. After 50 yards ignore another track which forks away to the right. Instead, pass the entrance to the Pitch and Putt course on your left and, almost immediately, pick up the start of Knightslow Wood. As the climb continues, extensive views over the northern area of the Cheshire Plain and the Mersey Valley open-up. On a clear day it is possible to pick out Winter Hill with its T.V. masts in the West Pennine Moors, north of Bolton.

The path eventually swings left to a tall ladder stile marking the entrance to Knightslow Wood. Beyond this the gradient levels out and in spring and early summer there is a continuous chorus of birdsong from robins, blue-tits, great-tits, blackbirds and thrushes. Only the ever-present jay contributes a discordant note.

A large gate, accompanied by a ladder stile, marks the further boundary of Knightslow Wood. Immediately in front of these turn sharp right onto the marked "Moorland Trail". This hugs the wall on your left as it winds through the trees.

After half a mile turn left over a stone stile to descend a short flight of steps onto a narrow path which clings to the crest of an embankment with a stream below on your left. By the next "Moorland Trail" sign fork left. Climb towards a square, roofless house, and stay to the left of the fences used during the annual Lyme Horse Trials. From this broad plateau there are views of, amongst other landmarks, Alderley Edge and Jodrell Bank. In season it is also the domain of the meadow pippit and the cuckoo.

By a small outcrop of rock, overlooking the confluence of two streams, swing right, with the path, for the gradual descent to a wide chatter track. Turn left along this for an easy 400 yards to West Park gate and

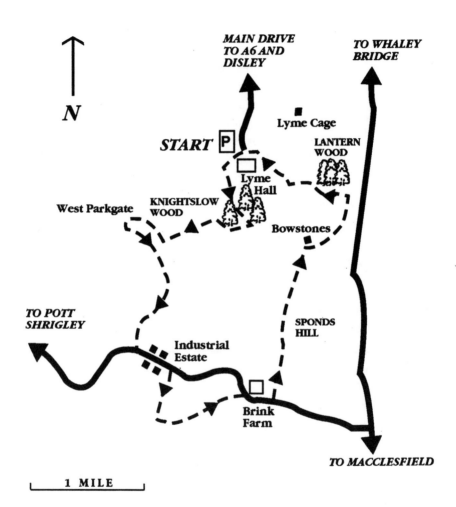

West Lodge. Through the gate, turn left over a bridge, proceeding along the track until it forms a junction with Shrigley Road by the Methodist Chapel at Green Close. Pass in front of the chapel before making a sharp turn left into a lane running alongside. This rises gradually to pass one or two houses on its way to a gated stile.

Beyond, stay to the right of a wall as the path narrows to pass through a small gate. Follow it leftwards across a small stream and stay with it as it strikes across rough pasture to meet Moorside Lane, some 100 yards to the west of Moorside Cottage. Over the stone step stile, turn right into the lane, pass Keeper's Cottage and proceed for well over half a mile to emerge onto the Pott Shrigley to Kettleshulme road. Turn left along the road, passing through the tiny industrial estate which now occupies the site of the former Pott Shrigley brickworks.

In a little under half a mile turn right over the stile with a footpath sign alongside. Climb steeply to the left of a drystone wall. After 100 yards the gradient eases as the path keeps to the right-hand side of a large field and, having passed through a gateway, maintains direction across the next field to arrive at a stone stile by a five-barred gate at Andrew's Knob. Do not climb over the stile. Instead turn left so cornering the same field with some fine views of the Torrs and of White Nancy to your right. One of the famous landmarks of East Cheshire, White Nancy is a small column with a rounded top which is painted white. It was constructed on the crest of Kerridge Hill to celebrate the victory of Waterloo in 1815.

Reaching the next corner of the field, turn right along a chatter track, cross over a cattle grid and, within ten yards, veer left along a narrow path to a stile which has the letter, F. P. painted alongside in white. Pass through a scattering of wind-blown trees and, at the next wall junction, swing slightly to your left, so keeping a broken wall on your right. Some tiny rock outcrops are set into the bank on your left. Confirmation that you are on the correct route is to be found on the first tree which carries the waymark of the Gritstone Trail. This is a letter "G" set into a boot.

Soon a small disused quarry is passed on your left. There the path broadens into a track, swings to the right around a pond and continues across a couple of fields to reach the Pott Shrigley road by Brink Farm. Exercising caution, turn right along the narrow road. After 300 yards, turn left over a stile which also bears the Gritstone Trail waymark.

The subsequent broad track climbs steeply for 100 yards to a stile adjacent to a five-barred metal gate. Beyond this the climb is long and steady but in summer it is almost impossible to miss the darting swifts as they fly overhead.

At the crest of Sponds Hill, at 410 metres above sea level, turn right off the track to a viewfinder. Erected in 1975 by the Council for the Protection of Rural England to mark European Architectural Heritage Year, it lists some of the summits visible on clear days. These include Winter Hill to the north, Kinder Scout to the east, the Berwyns and Clwydian hills in Wales and the Wrekin and Long Mynd in Shropshire. Having satiated yourself with these grand vistas, continue along the bridleway as it stays level for more than half a mile to reach Bowstones. These stand in small railed enclosure on your left.

Maintain your line of direction beyond Bowstones as the track acquires a hard surface and descends steeply to Dissop Head. After a half a mile, and with a white house on your right, turn left over a stile indicated by a Peak and Northern Footpath Society sign.

The path climbs the first field to a stile after which it traverses open moorland while staying a little to the right of a broken wall. After 100 yards it swings to the left to pass through a wall gap and then resumes the former direction through a patch of reeds.

It heads for an obvious stone step stile in the drystone wall at the top of the facing slope. Over the stile continue forward to the left of a wall. Down below is the first glimpse of Lyme Hall while, to the right, stands Lyme Cage.

Descend steeply with Lantern Wood on your right and then swing away to the left while still losing height rapidly. The path eventually swings round to meet Lantern Wood again at the far corner before passing through a gate in the facing wall. This leads into a section of the garden area of Lyme Park. The broad track passes through two more large black metal gates before arriving at a metalled estate road. Turn left along this for the descent to the ornate wrought-iron fence and gates at the front of the Hall. Afterwards continue down the steps to the car park.

10. Chatsworth House

Apart from one steep climb, the is an easy walk on riverside, woodland and field paths.

Route: Calton Lees car park – Beeley Lodge – Swiss Lake – Hunting Tower – Chatsworth House – Calton Lees car park.

Distance: 5 $^1/_2$ miles.

Start: Calton Lees car park. Map Reference 259684

Map: "The Peak District, White Peak Area", Number 24 in The Ordnance Survey's Outdoor Leisure series.

By Bus: There are buses from Matlock, Bakewell, Sheffield, Buxton, Rochdale and Ilkeston on summer Sundays and Bank Holidays. There is a very infrequent service, not even daily, from Bakewell midweek.

By Car: Calton Lees car park is signed from the B6012 road between Rowsley and Baslow.

Refreshments: Kiosk at Calton Lees serves light refreshments and drinks. Carriage House Restaurant at Chatsworth House serves meals and light refreshments. Both are open from 10.15 to 17.30 hours when Chatsworth House is open. Otherwise the nearest places for refreshments are Baslow and Edensor.

Chatsworth House

The choice of the site for Chatsworth House was apparently made by that redoubtable Elizabethan character, Bess of Hardwick who lived from 1520 to 1607. A wealthy widow by the age of 15, she soon married William Cavendish who had grown wealthy in the service of King Henry VIII, by helping to close down the monasteries. Having chosen the site, Bess had the original house built. This was magnificent by the standards of the period but faced the opposite way to the present one.

It was completed in 1555 but her grandson, William Cavendish, who had been created Duke of Devonshire for supporting William of Orange, built a newer, grander house between 1686 and 1708, even though he was plagued by some poor architects. In the 1820s the sixth Duke added the North Wing and made other minor alterations.

The gardens were landscaped by Capability Brown. People living nearby were moved to the newly-built villages of Edensor and Pilsley so the Duke's view would not be impaired. Paxton designed both villages and the Chatsworth conservatory. Later he planned Crystal Palace. With its fountains playing throughout the summer and its various gardens, Chatsworth has been described as "The Palace of the Peak".

The only part of Bess of Hardwick's Chatsworth still remaining is the Hunting Tower which stands in the woods high above the house. As its name suggests, it was for ladies and other spectators to watch the progress of the hunt. This is not the place to single out individual items but Chatsworth is a house full of artistic treasures and well repays of tour of the interior. There is also a farm which may be visited.

Chatsworth House

The Walk

Leave Calton Lees car park by the main entrance. Turn left along the B6012 for 15 yards. Pass through a white gate alongside the cattle grid before taking the footpath on the right. Descend the slope to pass to the right of a derelict stone building (an old mill) to meet the riverside path. Turn right so walking downstream with the River Derwent on your left.

A metal kissing gate permits access to the B6012. Turn left. Cross the narrow bridge controlled by traffic lights. 100 yards beyond, where the road bends sharply to the right, make a left turn into a metalled lane.

This is lined on either side by the blue and mauve flowers of the meadow cranesbill and red campion. The lane climbs steeply. By the farm at Beeley Hilltop the lane loses its surface and develops into a rough track.

50 yards beyond the final farm building, turn left over a stone step stile with a footpath sign. The path, which is a concessionary one created by the Chatsworth Estate, heads towards Baslow and Robin Hood. Over the next stile turn through 45 degrees to the right, crossing the field diagonally to an obvious step stile in the facing wall. Over this, turn left along the distinct path waymarked with a white arrow. Climb diagonally up the flank of the hill which is clothed in bracken.

There are some boggy stretches, some of which have been provided with duckboards. In summer this hillside is alive with swallow and meadow pippit. After a quarter of a mile the gradient increases for the final sharp, but mercifully short, pull to the summit.

At a T-junction formed by the path and wider track, turn left to a step stile adjacent to a gate. At the next T-junction, after 100 yards, go right to arrive at a cross roads in the path network. Continue forward, the track passing through coniferous woodlands mixed with rhododendron. As the track swings round towards the right a wide panorama opens-up but, after a short bend to the left, the woods close in once again.

At the next junction turn left to pass Swiss lake on your right. Look out, too, for the Swiss-type chalet across the water. At the next junction the track corners Emperor Lake, designed by Paxton to supply the

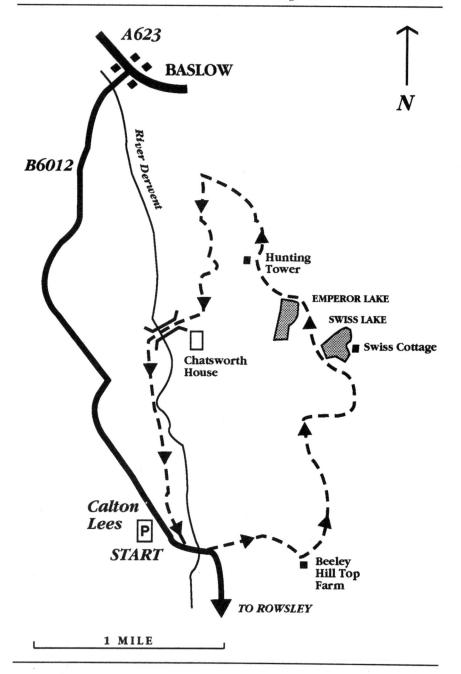

Chatsworth Fountain. These were created at the instigation of the sixth Duke of Devonshire who expected a visit from the Tsar of Russia which never materialised. He had served as our Ambassador in St. Petersburg and, on seeing the Tsar's fountain, decided to outshine him at Chatsworth.

A little way beyond Emperor Lake the track arrives at a telegraph pole. Turn left onto a narrow path to gain the Hunting Tower within a few yards. It overlooks Chatsworth Park and provides excellent views of the Derwent Valley with Edensor church very conspicuous. The iron cannon outside the Hunting Tower came from a vessel which fought at Trafalgar in 1805 and they were last fired at a celebration held at Chatsworth in 1926.

From the tower retrace your steps to the main track and turn left. After 75 yards, at a T-junction, turn right. Continue for a quarter of a mile until reaching a wooden footpath finger post on the left with two arms.

Turn left along the path signed to Baslow. Descend rapidly through the trees. Soon the path widens before arriving at a flight of steps. Descend these and continue in the same line direction across the parkland to meet a broad track. Turn left along this, staying with it until it reaches a stile alongside a gate. Do not climb over.

Instead turn right down the grassy slope to reach another broad track. Turn left again. By the main car park at the northern end of Chatsworth House veer right onto the main driveway which leads to the splendid stone bridge spanning the River Derwent.

At the far end make a left turn onto the path which traverses the parkland with the Derwent on your left and the House beyond. Where the river bends sharply, veer right to walk along the top of a raised bank or terrace until meeting the B6012 yet again.

Turn left along the road, pass through the white gate and cross to regain Calton Lees car park.

11. Haddon Hall

This route is a pleasant mixture of steep climbs, riverside and field paths through some delectable scenery in the White Peak.

Route: Youlgreave – Bradford Dale – Alport – Haddon Hall – Over Haddon – Meadow Place Grange – Youlgreave.

Distance: 9 ¹/₂ miles.

Start: Free car park at the western end of Youlgreave village. Map reference 206641

Map: "The Peak District, White Peak Area", number 24 in the Ordnance Survey's Outdoor Leisure series.

By Bus: There is a daily bus service to Youlgreave from Bakewell. Does not run on Sundays. Service number 181 runs every Sunday throughout the year from Coal Aston, Castleton and Bakewell.

By Car: Youlgreave may be reached from either Parsley Hay or Newhaven on the A515 Buxton to Ashbourne road. From the A6 take the signed minor road just south of Haddon Hall.

Refreshments: Pubs and cafes in Youlgreave and Over Haddon. Haddon Hall restaurant (self-service) opens from 11.00 hours to 17.30 between April 1 and October 1, except for Mondays and Sundays in July and August.

Haddon Hall

Haddon Hall is a much more modest affair than nearby Chatsworth. Whereas Chatsworth is grandiose in appearance, Haddon is much less overpowering. There has been a house on the site since Norman times when it was given to William Peverel, the builder of the castle at Castleton. In time, it passed to the Avenel family and then to the Vernons. The marriage of Dorothy Vernon to John Manners led to the property passing into the hands of the Masters family, then Earls and later Dukes of Rutland.

Again unlike Chatsworth, it has escaped remodelling or even extensions. This lucky escape was the result of the Dukes of Rutland leaving Haddon in 1640, to make Belvoir Castle their principal residence. As a consequence, Haddon is regarded as one of the finest examples of a medieval manor house, not only in the Peak District but in the country as a whole.

A tour of the house will reveal a treasure house of history, especially a considerable amount from the sixteenth century. The charge for admission is £3.20 for an adult and £1.90 for children with reductions for senior citizens.

Haddon Hall

The Walk

From the car park on the western end of Youlgreave village turn right along the road for approximately 100 yards before turning left through a squeezer stile alongside a five-barred gate. 50 yards after the second stile, and by the gable end of a derelict house, the path forms a T-junction with a broader path. Turn left to cross the wide stone bridge spanning the River Bradford. At the far end turn left again onto a riverside path which forms part of the Limestone Way. Within 100 yards negotiate a small metal gate to continue walking downstream with the river on your left.

The crystal-clear water allows glimpses of trout swimming below the surface and supports a population of mallard, coot and moorhen. Occasionally, you will catch sight of the dipper flexing his legs on top of a boulder or stone midstream as he bobs up and down before plunging into the water. In spring and early summer, the woods are filled with birdsong. The grey wagtail is abundant.

After a mile, turn left over a stone clapper bridge and, at the other end, turn right through a squeezer stile. At this point it is possible to pause for refreshments at Meadow Cottage which enjoys a spectacular view down Bradford Dale. Otherwise continue downstream, with the river now on your right, reaching a squeezer stile very close to another clapper bridge after a quarter of a mile. Ignore the bridge.

Stay forward to pass four stone cottages on your left before reaching a narrow road. Cross directly onto a broad track which soon swings left to pass beneath a small limestone crag to arrive at a packhorse bridge. Turn left over the stone bridge before climbing a walled lane lined with meadow cranesbill. Another road is reached after 250 yards.

Turn right for 50 yards and then turn right onto a path signed to Alport. This passes through clumps of elder and hawthorn before gaining a squeezer stile. From there aim for a limestone cliff on your right before swinging left to a wall gap. Maintain direction to a wall corner on the left. Round this before veering to your right towards an obvious squeezer stile in the facing wall which lines another road.

Turn right along this for the short distance into Alport village. Cross over the River Bradford, pass Rock House and look for the notice on the

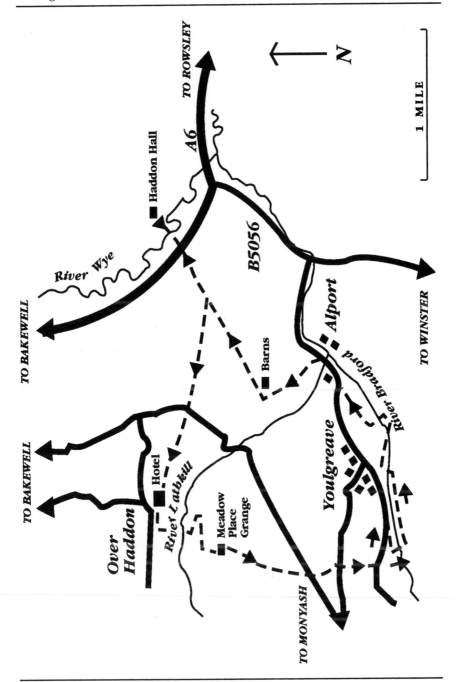

wall of a barn on the far side of the road which reads,

"NOTICE TO ALL VAGABONDS FOUND LODGING OR LOITERING OR BEGGING WITHIN THIS HAMLET WILL BE TAKEN UP AND DEALT WITH AS THE LAW DIRECTS. "

A few yards beyond this interesting notice turn left into a lane signed as a cul-de-sac and "Unsuitable for motors". Climb steeply for half a mile, to reach a complex of barns on the right. Stay to the left of these and negotiate two five-barred gates in quick succession. Immediately after the second turn right onto a path which is just to the left of a stone wall. There follows some really excellent walking on grass across a large field. Continue along the same line through gates and stiles to reach the A6 opposite Haddon Hall.

After your visit, re-cross the A6 to follow the same path as on the outward route until reaching a finger post in the centre of a large meadow. There, turn right onto another path signed to Wigger Dale. After 200 yards fork left onto a vague path which heads towards a roofless barn. In early summer beware of nesting lapwing. Walk to the left of the barn and also of a large hollow which follows a stone step stile in the field corner. Continue forward with a wall on your right, and after passing a gateway in the wall after 400 yards, veer to the left across the field corner to a footpath sign. By the sign is a stone step stile with very little room for big feet.

Maintain the line of direction for 50 yards to a squeezer stile which permits access to the road from Bakewell to Conksbury Bridge. Cross this, more or less directly, to a squeezer stile before heading over the field while veering a few degrees to the left and aiming for another stone step stile in the facing wall.

Over that, stay forward with a wall on your right and pass through a gateway while aiming for another footpath sign by the far field boundary. There, climb a stile over a wire fence followed by a stone step stile in a wall within one yard of each other. Keep an oddly-shaped tree on your left to negotiate another squeezer stile by the Haddon Hotel. Keeping the hotel on your right, advance to a road junction. Go left to another junction within 50 yards and turn left again before walking through the village of Over Haddon.

By the car park make a left turn into the road which descends steeply to the River Lathkill by Lathkill Lodge. Cross the stone clapper bridge and then turn left up a wide track running through Lathkill National Nature Reserve which is owned by English Nature and is noted for yellow archangel. Leaflets may be obtained from the Site Manager, Manor Barn, Over Haddon, Bakewell, Derbyshire, DE4 1JE.

Climb the track up the wooded slope and pass through a five-barred gate after which there is a fine view across the valley to Over Haddon.

Clapper Bridge, Bradford Dale

Beyond, turn sharp left, heading towards Meadow Place Farm. Pass through another gate with a sign to Youlgreave and Middleton, walk through the farmyard to a second gate, cross the large square in front of the impressive farmhouse to a stone step stile by a five-barred gate and then walk between two walls to a facing gateway with another footpath sign.

Go right, keeping to the left of a wall, following the path signed to Middleton. After 100 yards, and by a finger post, fork left to follow a series of yellow waymarker posts over open pasture. Soon a succession of step stiles will bring you to the road linking Conksbury with Parsley Hay. Cross to a stone step stile with a finger post alongside before advancing over the next field for 50 yards to another stile by the edge of a small wood where harebells proliferate.

Within another 20 yards another stile is reached. Continue forward over the next field to a squeezer stile and another road. Cross to another squeezer stile, advance with a wall on your immediate left for 30 yards, pass through a gateway with a redundant stile alongside, and then continue with a wall now on your left to a squeezer stile and, still with the wall on your left, reach another stile with a footpath finger post.

This permits access to another road. Turn left to regain the car park from which you started within a quarter of a mile.

Meadow Plae Grange, above Lathkill Dale.

12. Ilam Hall

A stiff climb is rewarded by the views and followed by a gentle stroll along the bank of the River Manifold.

Route: Ilam Hall – St. Bertram's Well – Beechenhill Farm – Castern Hall – Ilam Lodge – Ilam Hall.

Distance: 4 1/2 miles.

Start: Car park, Ilam Hall. Map reference 132506

Map: "The Peak District, White Peak Area", Number 24 in the Ordnance Survey's Outdoor Leisure series.

By Bus: Ilam is served by a daily service from Ashbourne. On summer Sundays and Bank Holidays there are buses from Macclesfield, Buxton, Mansfield and Derby. There is a service from Leek on Wednesdays.

By Car: Ilam is signed opposite Tissington Park Gates on the A515, a few miles north of Ashbourne.

Refreshments: Meals and drinks are served at the restaurant at Ilam Hall.

Ilam Hall

During the Middle Ages the land now surrounding Ilam Hall and the village was owned by the great Benedictine Abbey of Burton-upon-Trent. The antiquity of Ilam's history, however, may be gauged by the presence of the Saxon Cross in the churchyard and the "Battlestone" which is to be found on the riverside walk.

When the monasteries were dissolved by King Henry VIII in 1539, the estate became the property of John Port. It remained with his family until 1809 when it was transferred to David Pike-Watts. His daughter, Mary, married Jesse Watts-Russell who was responsible for building the hall that we see today.

His architect was James Trubshawe who designed on the grand scale, perhaps in imitation of Alton Towers, then owned by the Earl of Shrewsbury. Ilam had big formal rooms, high towers, ornamental chimneys and parapets.

In 1875, the hall passed to the Hanbury family who occupied it until 1927. Thereafter, for a short period, it became a restaurant before finally passing into the ownership of the National Trust for use as a Youth Hostel. The hall as it is today represents only a section of the original for it was partly demolished after 1927. Although the hall is not open to the public, the National Trust has developed the grounds into a country park with several walks.

Saxon Cross, Ilam

The Battlestone

Standing beside the riverside path, the Battlestone is the shaft of a Saxon cross said to date from an unrecorded battle near Ilam between the Danes and Saxons.

Church of the Holy Cross

Standing directly in front of Ilam Hall, the church of the Holy Cross is of very ancient origin. The Saxon shrine of St. Bertram is to be found inside. The church was substantially changed in 1618 and then, in the nineteenth century, it was restored by Gilbert Scott. There is also a Saxon cross in the churchyard.

Ilam Hall

St. Bertram

St. Bertram was a local hermit in the early Middle Ages who lived in a nearby cave. The bridge named after him in the grounds of Ilam Hall formerly carried the road from Ilam to Blore over the River Manifold. Later a new bridge was built a little downstream but St. Bertram's was restored in 1839.

Ilam Village

The village was largely re-built in the mid-nineteenth century by the Watts-Russell family, many of the houses and the village school constructed in the style of Swiss chalets.

Ilam Monument

The tall slender and elaborately carved monument which stands at the road junction in the centre of Ilam village was built in honour of Mary, wife of Watts-Russel during the nineteenth century.

The Walk

From the National Trust car park, walk down the drive of Ilam Hall for a few yards before veering right onto the path which passes to the left of the church. Where this ends at a metal kissing gate, turn left along a track. Beyond the next kissing gate turn right for 20 yards and then right again for another 20 yards along the hall drive.

Ilam Church

Turn right for the village centre. By the tall monument at the road junction go left into the road signposted to Dovedale and Thorpe. A few yards beyond the last house on your left, and by the village sign, turn left through a small wooden gate identified by a wooden footpath sign.

Fork left immediately, onto a path which climbs for about 25 yards to meet a broad track by a Peak and Northern Footpath Society sign. Cross this track directly onto a path heading, ultimately for Stanshope. Soon there is a small lake on your left. By a five-barred gate stay to the right,

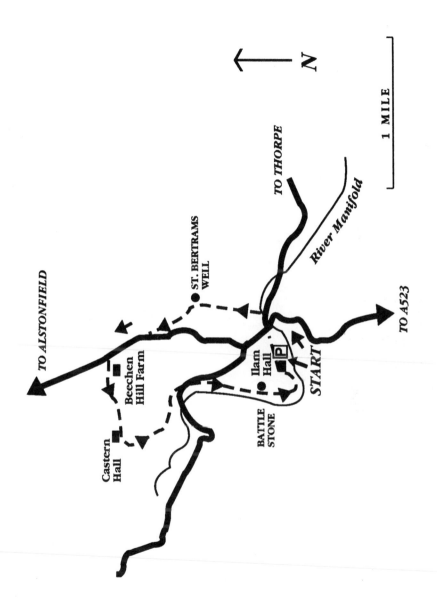

Ilam Monument

as signed by the National Trust, before embarking on a long gradual climb with a wall on your left.

The scenery is superb. Bunster Hill, on your immediate right, is a green rounded monster while to your left is the valley of the River Manifold with more gently rising hills and ridges beyond. Pass St. Bertram's Well, a small rocky hole under a solitary oak tree with water flowing from it. Continue uphill. Just beyond, at a Y-junction fork right before eventually turning left over a stile.

After a level stretch, start climbing again while aiming for the corner of Moor Plantation. Beyond the trees, ignore a stile and footpath sign close by on your left. Instead swing towards the right while staying close to a wall on your left. Almost at once you will pass a small abandoned quarry on your right, recognised, too, by its spoil heaps. Beyond, veer slightly to your right towards a stile, some 20 yards to the left of a gateway.

Stay forward to cross a broad track leading to Ilam Tops Farm before reaching a stone step stile and the road from Ilam to Alstonefield. Turn right along this, for a quarter of a mile noticing a now-defunct concrete platform by a farm entrance, once used for leaving churns of milk to be collected on their way to the dairy. Tankers have replaced them.

Turn left into the drive leading to Beechen Hill Farm, easily recognised by the name-plate and a small post box. Immediately before the first buildings, as directed by a sign, turn right through a metal five-barred

Ilam with Bunster Hill to the right.

gate, turn left by the barn corner and pass behind the farm house to reach a squeezer stile in the left-hand corner by another five-barred gate.

Stay to the right of a wall over the field to another squeezer stile before turning sharply to your left to descend a large sloping field to a stile in the bottom wall. Over that, veer through 45 degrees to your right down another sloping field to a five-barred gate in the corner by Castern Hall.

Turn left down the surfaced driveway, losing height rapidly to reach a road. Turn left, cross a cattle-grid and pass to the left of Ilam Lodge before turning right through metal gates onto a path. Do remember to place one new penny into the obvious collecting box.

With the dried-up River Manifold on your right negotiate two stiles in succession, both with doggy gates, before passing through a metal squeezer stile. Ignore a footbridge to your right, continuing along the path now known as "Paradise Walk". This Victorian name dates from the time when the Watts-Russel family laid out the gardens of the Hall.

There are several landmarks on the next section including "The Battlestone", "The Boil Holes" where the Manifold reappears after running underground from Wetton Mill, and "Congreve's Grotto", a stone bench and table beneath a limestone overhang where the dramatist is believed to have penned his play, "The Old Batchelor". Continue along the path beside the river until reaching "St. Bertram's Bridge". There turn left for the car park in front of Ilam Hall.

Packhorse Bridge, Ilam Hall.

13. Errwood Hall

The walk follows a mixture of field and moorland paths combined with a track alongside a reservoir.

Route: Whaley Bridge – Taxal Edge – Windgather Rocks – Pym Chair – Errwood Hall – Fernilee Reservoir – Whaley Bridge.

Distance: 9 miles

Start: Car park and lay-by on the west side of the A 5004 Whaley Bridge to Buxton road about half a mile south of Whaley Bridge. Map reference 008799.

Map: "The Peak District, White Peak Area", number 24 in the Ordnance Survey's Outdoor Leisure series.

By Rail: Whaley Bridge station, one mile north of the start of this walk, is served at half-hourly intervals on weekdays by trains from Buxton and Manchester. There is a limited service on Sundays.

By Bus: Transpeak, Manchester to Nottingham via Stockport, Buxton, Matlock and Derby stops at Whaley Bridge station. Daily including Sundays. Whaley Bridge is also served by local services from Stockport, Buxton, Macclesfield and New Mills. On summer Sundays and Bank Holidays there is a service from Glossop and Huddersfield.

By Car: The start is on the A 5004 Whaley Bridge to Buxton road which leaves the A6 at the traffic lights at Horwich End, Whaley Bridge.

Refreshments: Cafes and pubs serving bar meals in Whaley Bridge.

Errwood Hall

Today the upper reaches of the Goyt Valley, cradled by seemingly endless expanses of rolling moorland some four miles from Buxton, have the appearance of a true wilderness area. Errwood Hall lies in ruins. Yet, less than a century ago, this valley was home to a small, but thriving community complete with its own school and even a one-man coal mine.

Errwood Hall dated from the first half of the nineteenth century when it was built by the Grimshawe family who had prospered in the textile industry in Lancashire. Devout Roman Catholics they had their own private chapel and resident priest.

On the day of the chapel's consecration by the Bishop of Shrewsbury more than 200 people were present. The family also had its own private graveyard, on the hillside above the house, which may still be visited. It was abandoned in 1930, when the estate was purchased by the then Stockport Corporation for the construction of Errwood Reservoir.

The Grimshawe's were fervent travellers and were responsible for planting many species of exotic trees and shrubs in the grounds, including the rhododendron which still attract visitors in late spring.

The Shrine

A most unusual shrine is passed on that section of the route between Pym Chair and Errwood Hall. It is a small, circular building with a

Errwood Shrine, Goyt Valley.

conical roof. Inside there is a tiny stone altar backed by a tiled plaque depicting St. Joseph to whom it is dedicated. Even today it is very unusual to go inside without finding a spray of fresh flowers. It was built by the Grimshawes to the memory of Mrs. Grimshawe's companion and housekeeper, Miss Dolores.

Pym Chair

The origin of this name is obscure. One theory is that Pym was a religious teacher of the Non-conformist persuasion who sat on a rock there while addressing his congregation. Another suggests that John Pym, the great Parliamentarian leader, may have sat on a rock there while passing by.

Taxal

Taxal church tower has only one clock face, which looks away from the village.

The Walk

Leave the lay-by by the gate in the wall. Descend the path to cross the River Goyt by the bridge before climbing the lane which runs to the left of the church to reach the minor road through Taxal village. Turn left for a few yards but, opposite Glebe Farm and by the far corner of the Rectory, make a right turn over a stile onto a path signed to "Taxal Edge and Kettleshulme".

Stay close to the right-hand boundary of the field to a stone step stile in the facing wall. Continue directly ahead to a squeezer stile followed, almost at once, by a ladder stile. When the gradient eases, continue along the same line of direction but now with a wall on your left. Beyond the next stile cross the middle of a field, aiming for a very conspicuous ladder stile. Cross the narrow road to re-start climbing along a woodland ride which passes through a narrow belt of coniferous trees.

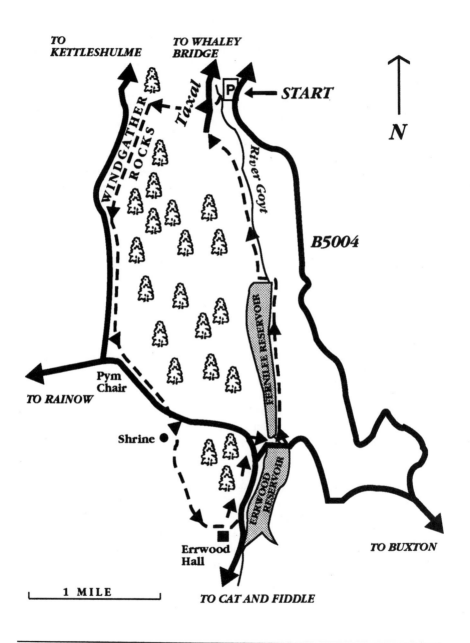

TO
KETTLESHULME

TO WHALEY
BRIDGE

Taxal

P   ← START

N

WINDGATHER ROCKS

River Goyt

B5004

Pym
Chair

TO RAINOW

Shrine ●

Errwood
Hall

TO BUXTON

1 MILE

TO CAT AND FIDDLE

After leaving these, and about half way up the slope, veer gradually to your right, taking direction from a stile in the facing wall. Do not climb over. Turn sharp left along the obvious path which traverses the crest of Taxal Edge.

When a broader path joins from your left, stay forward alongside a wall to a small wooden gate and then maintain your line of direction over the bottom end of an upland pasture. Beyond Clough Farm, which is a short distance away on your right, enter a plantation to a ladder stile. Over this, there is a wall on your right. Turn the corner with the wall but, over another ladder stile, turn left to walk the broad, grassy path which runs almost along the edge of Windgather Rocks, affording some far-reaching views of the East Cheshire hills and beyond.

Continue along this path as it approaches the minor road linking Kettleshulme with the Goyt Valley. Do not join the road. Climb another ladder stile and follow the concessionary path which heads towards Pym Chair car park. You do not go so far, however. Where a broken wall comes in from the left, and by a wooden stile on your right, fork left onto a clear path which runs along by a row of fencing posts, most of which have lost their wire. In approximately a quarter of a mile this reaches a ladder stile. Over this, turn left onto another concessionary footpath which runs alongside the road, separated from it by a broken-down stone wall.

Stay with this for half a mile. By a wooden finger post, signing Errwood Hall, turn right across the road and then onto a well-trodden path which runs across a short stretch of open moorland. At the first junction fork right, soon arriving at the shrine which is surrounded by trees. Continue along the path as it drops below Foxlow Edge to a cross-roads in the path network. Keep straight ahead, cross a stream by stepping stones and then climb high above. The narrow path soon widens as it approaches the ruins of Errwood Hall.

With the house on your right, stay with the track which was obviously once the main drive. At a T-junction turn left, descend slightly and then climb again. Where the track bends sharply round to the right, keep forward along a narrower path, negotiate a squeezer stile and descend through a field to the car park.

On reaching the road alongside Errwood Reservoir turn left and, using the pavement, head towards the embankment. At the road junction, turn right along the road signed to Buxton, cross the embankment to the far end, follow the road round to the left, and then make a left turn into the road which runs down the slope to Fernilee Reservoir.

At the bottom, climb the stile adjacent to a five-barred gate to follow the path along the eastern fringe of the reservoir. This was originally the track of the High Peak Railway which linked Whaley Bridge with Cromford. Turn left along the dam wall. At the far end turn right onto a broad track which runs above the River Goyt. Pass through a gate and advance 50 yards before veering to your right and keeping to the left of a drystone wall.

After 75 yards turn right through a gate and then left as indicated by an arrow. Keep a cottage on your left before swinging right by a telegraph pole to walk alongside a sparse hedge to a stile. Continue to a five-barred gate beyond which the path winds its way down the side of the valley to a footbridge spanning the stream in Mill Clough close to its confluence with the River Goyt. Stay forward for 20 yards to a stile, turn right for 5 yards and then turn left at once over another stile signed to Taxal.

Do not cross the footbridge over the Goyt but, staying to the left of a seat, keep forward to enter Park Wood, a nature reserve owned by the Derbyshire Wildlife Trust. Climb gently to a stile. On gaining open country walk to the left of a tree stump and then to the right of a solitary tree before striking out across meadowland on a clear path.

By the footpath sign, turn right along the lane to reach the village of Taxal where the outward route is joined for the final quarter of a mile.

14. Woodhead Chapel

A superb moorland walk with fine views mostly on clear paths and returning along the track of a former railway.

Route: Crowden – Lad's Leap – Bottoms Reservoir – Torrside – Crowden.

Distance: 10 miles

Start: Car park, Crowden. Map Reference 072994

Map: "The Peak District, Dark Peak Area", Number 1 in the Ordnance Survey's Outdoor Leisure series.

By Bus: Express service number 350 stops at Crowden. It serves Liverpool, Manchester, Sheffield, Chesterfield, Mansfield, Nottingham, Peterborough, Cambridge, Ipswich and Clacton.

By Car: Crowden in on the A 628 between Hollingworth and the Flouch Inn. The car park is signed.

Refreshments: None on the route.

Woodhead Chapel

The Chapel of St. James, Woodhead, is one of the most ancient of all ecclesiastical establishments in the Peak District National Park. The exact date of its foundation is unrecorded but it is known that the money was provided by Sir Edmund Shaa. A native of the locality, he had abandoned the poverty and hardships of moorland life to seek his fortune in London. There he did indeed discover that the pavements were lined with gold. He prospered and, in true Dick Whittington fashion, became Lord Mayor of the capital. In 1487, he bequeathed funds for the endowment of a resident priest at Woodhead but, following the Dissolution of the Monasteries in 1539, the annual stipend was diverted into the coffers of the Crown.

Woodhead Chapel.

Consequently, St. James's Chapel was always short of funds. By 1651, the annual income was thirty shillings (£1.50) and it was only a parish in its own right between 1860 and 1920. Otherwise it was served from either Mottram-in-Longdendale or Glossop.

The parish has never been blessed with a large population and today there are fewer than 40 people resident within a five-mile radius. The only exception was in the middle years of the nineteenth century when the Longdendale reservoirs were under construction and the railway tunnel was being driven under the moors between Woodhead and Dunford Bridge.

In 1849, at least 28 railway navvies died of cholera, 21 of them being buried in the churchyard of St. James's. The oldest part of the present building, the lower sections of the north wall, date from the early eighteenth century with other parts being either added or restored at later dates. For centuries, this tiny millstone grit building served as a landmark to the drivers of the packhorse trains which carried salt and other goods over the moors from Cheshire to Yorkshire by way of Saltersbrook Bridge.

Until the boundary changes in the 1970s, the Longdendale valley belonged the Cheshire. Sandwiched between Derbyshire to the south and Yorkshire to the north, it was known as "The Cheshire Panhandle". The county, apparently, wanted to keep a check on all the dues which had to be paid on the transported salt. Today, it is in Derbyshire and a welcome sight for weary ramblers coming off the surrounding moors after a long day's walking.

The Walk

Leave Crowden car park by taking the path signed to the toilets. By the toilet block, turn right to reach a cross roads by the campsite entrance after 100 yards. Turn left along a bridleway which is surfaced initially but which, after crossing a stone bridge, deteriorates into a track. The bridge is limited to 3 tons . . . so you have been warned!

50 yards beyond the bridge, pass through a small gate alongside a five-barred one, to climb gradually until reaching a Pennine Way sign. Make a right turn onto England's premier National Trail. The path is well-trodden as it heads up Crowden Brook which is flowing down below on your right.

At the end of half a mile climb a ladder stile before turning sharp left onto a narrower path which runs alongside a stone wall for the initial 50 yards. Then turn left again, through a wall gap, almost doubling back in direction. Climb steeply up the hillside to pass through one derelict wall before reaching a second within 40 yards. Do not pass through. Instead, make a sharp turn to the right, climbing still alongside a wall to emerge onto a vast expanse of open moorland. To your left there is no view but to your right the moors extend for miles so providing a real feeling of what the Dark Peak is really about.

After gaining the top the path runs to the right of a wall for a short distance but, where the wall ends, the gradient levels out. The path is clear and easy to follow as it traverses the top of Highstone Rocks to provide some exhilarating upland walking. At the end of about a quarter of a mile, another drystone wall goes off to the left while you pass a wooden stake close to your left. Having passed this, veer slightly to the

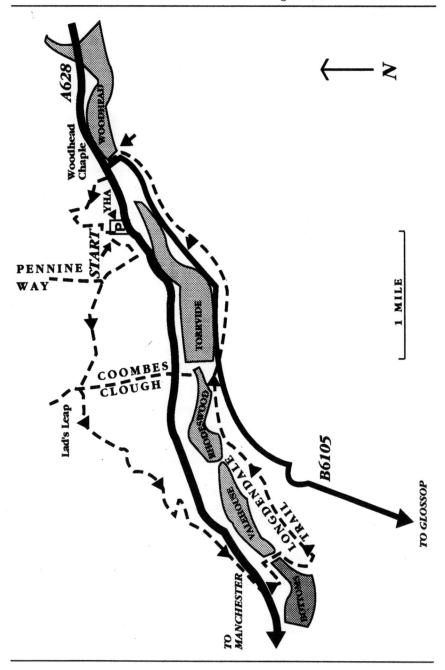

right, making for a small cairn of stones. This is the first of a series which are there to guide the walker closer and closer to the gritstone edge running above Coombes Clough.

To the south there is a clear view across Longdendale to Bleaklow and, some distance beyond, to that other great massif of the Peak District, Kinder Scout. To the west Werneth Low, crowned with radio masts, and Cown Edge are easy to recognise and, in the far distance, it is possible to pinpoint the eastern areas of Greater Manchester.

At the head of Coombes Clough, where it joins Hollins Clough, make a U-turn, fording the stream by Lad's Leap. Continue forward with Coombes Clough falling away sharply to your left until a very small abandoned quarry is reached. Pass to the right of this before leaving the main path by veering slightly left onto a narrow path to traverse a stretch of open moorland covered with bilberry and heather.

The path leads to an intersection in the path system identified by a tall ladder stile with footpath signs adjacent. Ignore the path signed to Arnfield. Climb the stile to embark on a long, steep descent, still on a narrow path. Caution is needed because of the precipitous drop on your left.

The path levels out and widens as it passes through the former quarry of Tintwistle Knarr. Stay with the broad track as it works its way through fields of boulders where natural regeneration has taken place since the workings were abandoned many years ago.

After passing a plantation on your left, climb a stile and continue forward, still losing height. At a Y-junction fork right and, a short distance beyond, ignore another track running off to the left. After a couple of U-turns, one to the left, the other to the right, the path heads directly down the slope to the A628 trunk road. However, about 150 yards short of meeting the road, the path forms a junction with a signed bridleway. Join this by making an acute turn to your right and staying to the right of a wall.

The bridleway climbs slightly to a metal gate and continues upwards for some distance before levelling to pass through another gate and reach the A628 by a tall, narrow stone house.

Turn right along the main road. Within a quarter of a mile, and by the entrance to Chapel Brow on your right, pass through a metal turnstile on your left to walk a field path as it arcs round to the right to another turnstile. Turn left along the narrow road running alongside Bottoms Reservoir, staying with it as it turns right to cross the embankment of Valehouse Reservoir.

At the far end of the embankment turn right, as directed by a footpath sign, to walk along the path on the southern flank of Bottoms Reservoir. Within a few yards negotiate a turnstile before continuing to a stone stile alongside some iron railings. 100 yards beyond, veer left onto an unsigned but distinct path which climbs up a field for 75 yards to a stile. Over that, go diagonally to your left, aiming for a small stone tunnel under the former Manchester to Sheffield railway line.

Pass through the tunnel and turn left immediately to join the new Longdendale Trail which has been converted from the former Manchester to Sheffield railway line and runs from Hadfield to Woodhead where further progress is now barred by a sealed tunnel entrance.

Continue along the Trail for several miles until reaching the eastern end of Torrside Reservoir. After a slight climb and after passing beneath some overhead power lines but before a smoke-blackened redbrick house, turn left off the trail to cross the embankment of Woodhead Reservoir. At the far end, where the road bends sharply to the right, turn left up a flight of steps to reach the A 628. At the top of the steps turn left along the road, using the pavement because there is heavy traffic.

By the far corner of the appropriately-named Bleak House, on the north side of the road, turn right onto a track which circles up the slope to meet the driveway to Woodhead Chapel. Turn right for a few yards if you wish to visit, although it is usually kept locked. The view from the churchyard makes the visit worthwhile. It includes not only the Bleaklow edges, but the Longdendale Valley almost up to the Yorkshire boundary at Saltersbrook Bridge.

From the chapel, retrace your steps for 40 yards and turn right over a ladder stile by a five-barred gate. Climb the steep, cobbled track. After a quarter of a mile, and just beyond a wall corner on the right, a T-junction is reached. Turn left onto another stoney track which contours just below the large spoil heap from a former quarry. As it arcs to the right there is another fine view, this time up Crowden Valley.

Having rounded the spoil heap and with a few wind-blown trees enclosed by a wooden fence 100 yards to your right, turn acutely to the left onto a grassy path. This descends the hillside steeply until forming a T-junction with a wider track at a point where a finger post points towards Open Country. Turn left along the track. It is less steep but still losing height. After 100 yards a ladder stile is reached. Over that turn left along the driveway to Crowden Outdoor Pursuits Centre which belongs to Rotherham Education Committee.

Continue forward through a five-barred gate, which is almost invariably open, to a cross roads. Stay forward to the toilet block and there make a final turn to your left to regain your starting point in Crowden car park.

15. Forest Chapel

A walk through the Forest of Macclesfield using paths and old bridleways, with steep climbs.

Route: Teggs Nose – Teggs Nose Reservoir – Clough House – Hardingland – Forest Chapel – Walker Barn – Teggs Nose.

Distance: 6 1/2 miles.

Start: Car park, Teggs Nose Country Park, near Macclesfield. Map Reference 960734

Map: "The Peak District, White Peak Area", Number 24 in the Ordnance Survey's Outdoor Leisure series.

By Bus: Buses from Macclesfield and Buxton on Saturdays and summer Sundays.

By Car: Teggs Nose Country Park is signed from the A537 Macclesfield to Buxton Road.

Refreshments: The kiosk at Teggs Nose is open on Sundays throughout the year, summer Saturdays and daily in school holidays in July/ August. It serves hot and cold drinks and light refreshments. The "Setter Dog" near Walker Barn offers bar meals from 12.00 to 14.00 hours.

Forest Chapel

Commonly known as "Forest Chapel", this remote place of worship is dedicated officially to St. Stephen. It is possible that a church or chapel has stood on the spot since Norman times because the surrounding area is all part of the Royal Forest of Macclesfield. It is certain, however, that a chapel was built here in 1673 for the use of local farmers and to obviate the necessity for them to travel into Macclesfield for Sunday worship. That first chapel was entirely rebuilt in 1834 from local millstone grit. That is the building we see today. Above the doorway are two carved stones, one of which bears the inscription "S. S. 1673". This a stone from the original chapel.

Forest Chapel

The Rushbearing Ceremony

The annual rushbearing ceremony is held on the first Sunday after August 12th when the chapel is decorated with plaited rushes cut from a local marshy spot. These are interwoven with flowers while other rushes are spread over the floor. This custom was once widespread. The rushes helped to keep the floor warm in the days before central heating. Each year they were cleared out to be replaced by new ones but in many cases the practice was abandoned after the plague.

The Walk

Leave Teggs Nose by the car park entrance, keeping to the left of the cattle grid. At the junction with the road make a left turn onto the wide track signed to Teggs Nose summit. After 150 yards, pass through a small gate and keep a wall on your right until reaching a wooden kissing gate. Beyond, ignore the summit sign. Instead make a left turn

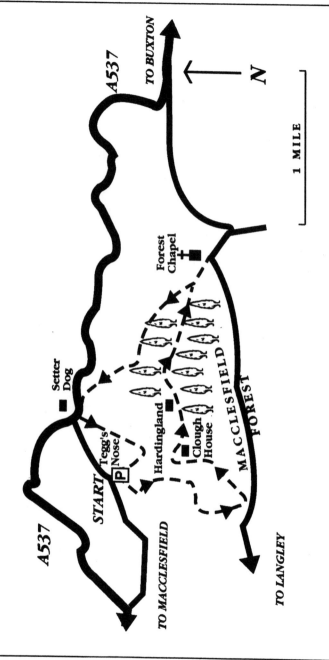

up a flight of steps before continuing on a former quarry track as it climbs the heather-covered slope to provide a panoramic view of Macclesfield Forest dominated by Shuttlingsloe, the so-called "Matterhorn of Cheshire". As the gradient levels, the track passes through the heart of Teggs Nose quarry where there is a crane and other industrial exhibits including a "jaw crusher".

Pass an enormous hole with a sheer rock face on your right. At the far end, where the track bends round to the right, continue forward onto a narrower path. This quickly widens as it, too, curves round to the right to reveal the communication tower on Croker Hill. About 100 yards beyond a Gritstone Trail waymarker (a boot with the letter 'G' in the middle) make a left turn over a stile and descend a small flight of steps followed by a line of flagstones. Where these end, continue downhill through gorse and bracken before descending a very long flight of steps with a Teggs Nose Country Park display panel at the bottom.

Negotiate a black metal kissing gate and turn right along the embankment of Teggs Nose Reservoir. At the far end turn left at the T-junction to follow a bridleway along the south side of the reservoir which is home to mallard, coot, moorhen and other wildfowl.

After the reservoir has been left behind the route is lined with lush vegetation which attracts meadow brown and tortoiseshell butterflies. Continue over a cattle grid and over a stile for a gradual climb before the gradient eases. By a small amount of wooden fencing, and by a Teggs Nose sign, veer left into the woods. After 50 yards use the stepping stones to cross a stream and climb to a wooden five-barred gate with another but smaller Teggs Nose sign fixed to it.

Resume climbing along this sunken lane to a five-barred gate with a stile alongside which forms part of the boundary of the country park. From there keep Clough House Farm on your right before gaining a narrow surfaced road by the farm entrance. Cross directly into another metalled lane which is signed to Forest Chapel. This drops into a valley but when it starts climbing, deteriorates into another lane or bridleway.

Stay with this walled lane as you pass to the left of Crooked Yard Farm. At the crest of the slope the lane passes through a ninety degree turn to the right, and drops to cross a stream before climbing beneath overhead wires to a T-junction.

The way ahead is very overgrown so turn left into another lane which has a wall on the left and a bank on the right where hawthorn and crab apple grow.

By Hardingland House Lane there is a junction with another narrow surfaced road. Turn right and, after 100 yards and, by a Peak and Northern Footpath Society sign, turn right over a stile into the forest.

With your feet now cushioned by fallen pine needles climb through the trees to a T-junction. Turn right along the path signed to Forest Chapel. You will soon pass Dimples, a barn with boarded-up windows, which is the relic of farm which occupied the site before North West Water established the present coniferous forest.

At the next path intersection continue forward onto a path signed to Forest Chapel. The going steepens considerably and the path becomes stepped for a long way before finally levelling-out to afford a good view of Shuttlingsloe, "The Cat and Fiddle" and the surrounding moorlands.

Over the next stile turn right along Charity Lane for a steep descent to Forest Chapel. But do not rejoice. You have to climb back again. After your visit to the chapel retrace your steps along Charity Lane, this time to the summit which is recognised by two bulbous satellite dishes. They stand at a height of 475 metres compared with Forest Chapel which is on the 300 metre contour.

From the summit there is a view which embraces Wildboarclough, "The Cat and Fiddle", the Torrs, Windgather Rocks and, in the far distance, the western edges of Kinder Scout.

At the next T-junction turn right along a surfaced lane which drops to meet the A537, Macclesfield to Buxton road. Turn left along the road. Ten yards before "The Setter Dog", turn left into another lane signed to Crooked Yard Farm. This again loses height quickly. After a mile, a Y-junction is reached. Fork right for a further steep drop into a valley followed by another short, steep climb.

As the gradient levels-out, and by the last in a series of telegraph poles which has a welcome seat at its base, turn right into Saddlers' Way, a cobbled track sporting red, blue and green waymarks.

Saddlers' Way climbs steeply to the car park at Teggs Nose.

16. Padley Chapel

A route along distinct paths through one of the beauty spots of the Peak District and visiting one of the National Trust's moorland estates.

Route: Grindleford station – Padley Chapel – Padley Gorge – Longshaw Lodge – Oaks Wood – Grindleford station.

Distance: 5 miles.

Start: Grindleford station. Parking along approach road. Map Reference 251788

Maps: 1) "The Peak District, White Peak Area", number 24 in the Ordnance Survey's Outdoor Leisure series; 2) "Sheffield", SK 28/38 in the Ordnance Survey's Pathfinder series.

By Rail: Grindleford is served by frequent trains midweek from Sheffield and Manchester. There is a restricted service on Sundays.

By Bus: Daily services, including Sundays, from Sheffield, Chesterfield, Buxton, Bakewell and Castleton. Buses from Ilkeston, Tideswell and Coal Aston on summer Sundays and Bank Holidays.

By Car: Grindleford station is signed from the B6251, Grindleford to Fox House road.

Refreshments: There is a cafe at Grindleford station and another at Longshaw Lodge. Pubs in Grindleford village serve bar meals. "The Fox House", just off the route, serves bar food.

Padley Chapel

Padley Chapel is the only extant portion of Padley Hall, a medieval manor house and home to the Fitzherbert family. At the time of the Reformation, they remained staunch Roman Catholics who gave shelter to priests.

In 1588, when persecution was at its height because of the Armada scare, two priests were arrested. They were Robert Ludlam and Richard

Garlick. Subsequently they were tried at Derby and hanged, drawn and quartered. James Fitzherbert, then master of Padley Hall, suffered a similar fate at a later date.

The present chapel was formerly the gatehouse. In 1933 it was bought by the Roman Catholic Diocese of Nottingham and restored as a shrine to the Padley martyrs. There is an annual pilgrimage on the Thursday nearest 12th July.

Padley Chapel

The Walk

After parking the car, continue in the same direction to pass the cafe on your right and then to cross over the railway bridge. Continue over a second bridge with white metal rails which spans Burbage Brook. Stay with the rough track for almost 400 yards passing some houses on your left to reach Padley Chapel.

Retrace your steps. Before re-crossing the railway bridge turn left through a squeezer stile with a National Trust sign adjacent. The path wends its way through Yarncliffe Woods, a mixture of broadleaved trees. If you are fortunate to come this way on a sunny summer day the flora will be dappled with light. Pass through a gap in an old broken wire fence to reach a T-junction.

Turn to the left, descend a small flight of steps to a footbridge over the brook. This is followed by a climb up a much longer flight of steps to a Y-junction. Fork left up a steep path which is stepped initially. At the next T-junction turn right. The gradient eases as the path clings to the contour above Burbage Brook which is below on your right. You will find many large pieces of millstone grit embedded in the path.

At the end of a long level stretch the path begins to climb gradually before reaching a small gate which gives access to open moorland country with views of Carl Wark and Higger Tor to your left. Ignore the first footbridge on your right. Continue alongside the brook to a second. Turn right over this and then immediately left up a stoney path.

At the next T-junction, after 150 yards, turn right to cross a tiny culverted stream before entering more mixed woodlands which have ample bracken. Leave the woods through a small wooden kissing gate to enjoy a fine view of Eyam edge in the distance. Head towards a gated stile which permits access to the B6521, "The Fox House" to Grindleford road.

Cross directly to pass through a white gate to follow the drive to Longshaw Lodge, a former hunting lodge owned by the Duke of Rutland but now in the ownership of the National Trust. Stay to the front of the house, pass through a small gate and, at the Y-junction, fork left to another small gate. The path initially keeps to the right of a

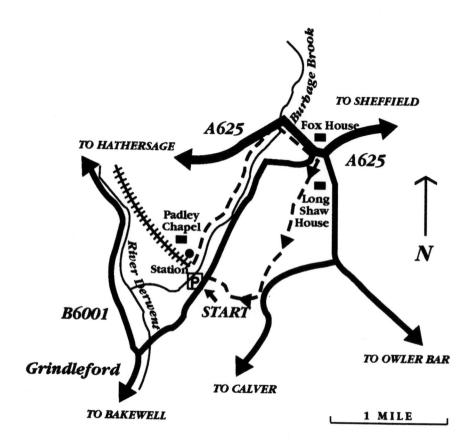

metal-barred fence beyond which are some rhododendrons.

Pass two large gateposts to reach a small wooden gate adjacent to a five-barred one, keeping forward with an open aspect. Soon, much closer to hand, you will have a wood on your left. Almost where this ends turn right to a stile which has its top at ground level because of the sunken wall. It is not easy to detect but, careful observation will reveal that it provides access to a flagged path heading directly over open ground to another wood.

From the point where the flagging ends, descend steeply through Oaks Wood, negotiate a small gate and continue to reach the road on the edge of Grindleford. Turn left. Immediately before the 40 mph sign, make an acute turn to the right onto a surfaced path signed to the station.

17. Charlotte Brontë

A short but demanding route which involves some steep climbing followed by a gentle return along field paths.

Route: Hathersage – North Lees – Stanage Edge – Dennis Knoll – Brontë Cottage – Hathersage.

Distance: 6 miles.

Start: Car park, Hathersage. Map Reference 232815

Map: "Sheffield", SK 28/38, Number 743 in the Ordnance Survey's Pathfinder series.

By Rail: Hathersage is served by frequent trains on the Manchester to Sheffield line. There is a restricted service on Sundays.

By Bus: Daily services from Sheffield, Castleton and Chesterfield. Buses from Coal Aston, Staveley and Chesterfield on summer Sundays and bank Holidays.

By Car: Hathersage is on the A625 Whaley Bridge to Sheffield road.

Refreshments: There is a selection of pubs serving bar meals and also several cafes.

Charlotte Brontë

Charlotte Brontë appears to have gained much of her background information for "Jane Eyre" during a visit to Hathersage in June and July, 1845, a year before she commenced writing her great novel. She was the guest of a former schoolfriend, Ellen Nussey, sister to the then vicar. During her three-week holiday she could not have failed to have noticed the prevalence of the name "Eyre" in and around Hathersage. The Eyre Brasses inside the church are outstanding. These show four couples with children dating from 1450. There are also the Eyre Windows and, in the churchyard, the Eyre graves. Indeed, during her stay, Thomas Eyre was buried there. She also visited North Lees Hall, then home of a Mrs. Mary Eyre.

In the novel, Jane Eyre flees to the village of Morton in the north Midlands. Morton figures on the Charity Boards inside the church. Also, on her arrival in Hathersage, Charlotte would have alighted from the stage coach at "The George Inn" where Thomas Morton was landlord. In the book, Morton also has some needle mills. So, too, did Hathersage at the time of Charlotte's stay whereas the mills of Haworth all produced wool. Jane Eyre took up an appointment as governess at Thornfield Hall, home of Mr. Rochester. The description of Thornfield is almost an exact mirror of North Lees Hall, just outside Hathersage. Indeed, there is little doubt that her portrait of an Apostles cupboard was inspired by one she saw at North Lees Hall. Today it is in the Brontë Museum at Haworth. By no strange coincidence, the first mistress of North Lees Hall, Agnes Ashurst, had been confined to an upstairs room with padded walls because she went insane and she died in a fire. It is literally the story of Mrs. Rochester in "Jane Eyre".

During her stay in Hathersage, Charlotte probably walked onto Stanage Edge and towards the former Moscar Cross. In those days it was painted white, an inspiration, perhaps for "Whitcross" in the book.

Little John's Grave, Hathersage.

Little John

Hathersage churchyard also boasts the grave of Little John, companion of Robin Hood. As nobody has yet proved the existence of Robin, it is equally difficult to substantiate this particular claim. In the nineteenth century, the grave was excavated and an enormous thigh bone brought to light. It was taken by many to give validity to the claim. Later the bone was re-interred.

There is also a strong tradition that Little John was a native of Hathersage and that, towards the end of his life, he retired there. It is worth remembering, too, that Robin Hood was often associated with the Forest of Barnsdale, which covered parts of Yorkshire and Derbyshire.

The Walk

Leave the car park by the public conveniences sign. Pass to the left of the Methodist Church to the A625. Cross to the Post Office. Proceed up Besom lane which is adjacent. At the end turn left into Baulk Lane.

Walk for approximately 100 yards. Turn right through a gate onto a path signed to the parish church. This is part of the Shuttleworth Memorial Trail, designed in memory of Lieutenant Commander John A. Shuttleworth in 1985. The well-maintained path keeps to the left of a wall. Beyond the first gate turn left for 5 yards and then turn right through another gate to walk through the churchyard.

Pass through the lych gate and turn left along a very narrow surfaced road for 100 yards. Where the road makes an acute turn leftwards, negotiate a facing stile. Turn right. By a large tree make another left turn down a slope to a stile in the left-hand corner of the field and then turn right over a stone footbridge.

Continue beneath some overhead power lines and along the left-hand field boundary, following a very distinct path. Beyond a crude squeezer stile, turn through 45 degrees to the right, aiming for another field corner. At the top of the gentle rise, turn left over a stile to join another path coming in from your right. This path levels out as it runs immediately to the right of a fence and a line of trees, with views of Stanage Edge in front.

Beyond a metal gate, veer right on a narrow path to the right of Cowclose Farm to reach a small gate. Continue forward along the contour with grass underfoot until the path arcs to the right and becomes more distinct. Within a short distance it reaches a stile and a narrow road.

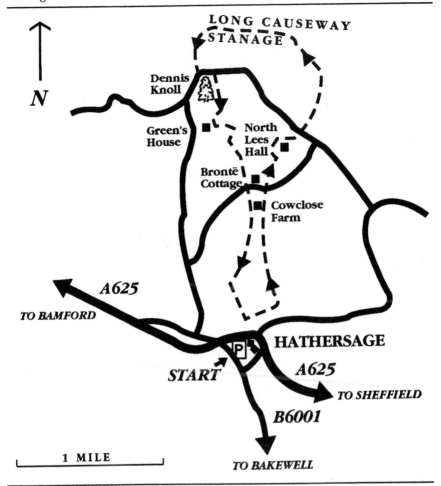

Turn left and, within 30 yards, turn right into NorthLees campsite. Keeping the office on your left, head for a small gate and continue to a squeezer stile. Maintain direction through the woods, with a stream on your left as the path begins to climb. Turn left over a small footbridge to a small gate before making a right turn to pass between two fences. Climb a stepped section of path to a small gate, followed within 5 yards by a squeezer stile. Stay forward, still climbing steps, to a T-junction with a bridleway. Turn right along this to pass just above North Lees Hall, with some good views southwards through the gaps in the trees.

A short distance before meeting a road, turn left onto an unsigned but clear path to reach a small stone building used by the mountain rescue team. Pass through another small gate, cross the road onto a broad path opposite and, after 250 yards, fork right at a junction, before using another small gate to gain entry to a plantation.

Leave the plantation by a gate followed by a stiff climb through the bracken, striking diagonally to your right until you emerge onto Stanage Edge itself. Admire the view and then turn left along the path known as "The Long Causeway". Pass a broken stile but, within a few yards, ignore a path to the right. Instead, stay with the broadening track to begin losing height, ignoring any side paths until reaching a road by a right-angled bend

Turn left along this road, following the direction signed to Ringinglow and having Denis Knoll Plantation on your right. By the far corner of this plantation, negotiate a stile alongside a cattle-grid and immediately turn right along the path signed to Green's House. It is a good turf path which makes for a welcome change after the Long Causeway. There is a wall on your right.

Beyond a stone step stile, the gradient increases. Pass through a gateway and turn left, still keeping the wall on your right. After the next stile, stay forward between two walls to a five-barred gate. Turn left along a farm track which passes between buildings to another five-barred gate. Notice that the landowners welcome careful walkers and the waymarks along this section have been provided by the Country Landowners' Association.

Beyond the gate immediately turn right through a squeezer stile onto a path hemmed in by two fences. Through the next squeezer stile maintain your line of direction across a field to two small gates set one foot apart in the wall. Take your choice before aiming for the right-hand corner of the next field to enter a wood. Descend to a footbridge over Hood Brook and, at the far end, turn right. The brook is now on your right.

Pass through a small gate, and follow the line of overhead power lines to a stone step stile by Birley Road, a little to the right of Brontë Cottage. Cross to a gate with a footpath sign and then simply follow the distinct path with a fence on your left. Keep Brookfield Manor House on your right, going forward between a fence and hedge.

Over the next stile cross the pasture to a clearly visible footpath sign. By this turn right along a broad track to reach Lane End House. Beyond the track becomes Baulk Lane, leading directly back into the centre of Hathersage.

Brontë Cottage

18. Well Dressing

A very easy walk with only one slight climb.

Route: Tissington – Townhead – Crakelow Farm – Tissington Trail – High Flats – Tissington.

Distance: 3 miles.

Start: National Park car park, Tissington. Map Reference 178521

Map: "The Peak District, White Peak Area", Number 24 in the Ordnance Surbey's Outdoor Leisure series.

By Bus: There are buses from Ashbourne and Hartington on Thursdays and Saturdays. On summer Sundays and Bank Holidays there are buses from Congleton, Newcastle, Macclesfield, Buxton, Mansfield and Derby.

By Car: Tissington village is signed from the A515 Buxton to Ashbourne road, about 3 miles north of Ashbourne.

Refreshments: Tea Rooms in Tissington village. Restricted opening in winter.

Well Dressing

This custom appears to be almost entirely confined to the Peak District. Its origins are obscure. Possibly it dates back to the pre-Roman period when thanksgivings were offered to the God of Water for the supplies found in the limestone area of the White Peak.

As with so many ancient customs and traditions, Well Dressing was absorbed by the early church, modified and given very strong religious associations. Little is known of the custom during the medieval period, but it was certainly practised at Tissington in the early seventeenth century, perhaps in gratitude for having survived a very severe drought in 1615.

A large wooden frame is soaked for several days and then covered with puddled clay. The design, which varies every year, is then pricked out

on the clay. The outline is normally filled with alder cones and then filled in with mosses, lichen and bark to provide a background. Finally, petals of wild and garden flowers are placed on top to add the colours which attract so many visitors. Traditionally, Tissington is always the first peak District village to hold its well dressing service, usually on Ascension Thursday.

Well Dressing, (Eyam)

The Walk

Leave by the car park entrance, taking the road into the centre of Tissington village. By the pond turn right, walking along the wide, grass-lined main street, passing the church on your right and the Hall on the left.

Continue to the far end of the village, leaving the houses behind. Where the road bends round to the left stay forward into a walled lane which ends at a five-barred gate after 100 yards. Maintain the line of direction, keeping a wall on your left as you traverse a large field to another gate, followed by a second. From there, the path becomes a walled lane again and climbs very slightly. In summer the route is lined with meadow cranesbill.

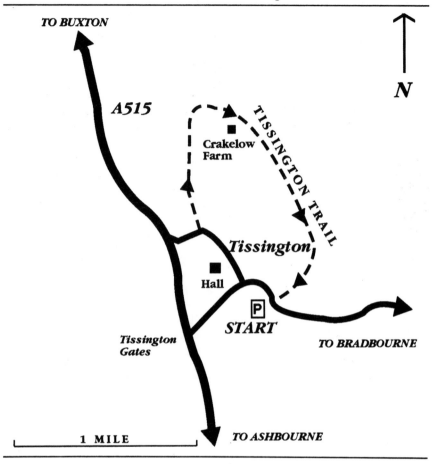

TO BUXTON

A515

N

Crakelow
Farm

TISSINGTON TRAIL

Tissington

Hall

START

Tissington
Gates

TO BRADBOURNE

1 MILE

TO ASHBOURNE

Within a further 100 yards the wall on your right veers away. Still advance with a wall on your left. After another 100 yards the path reverts to being a walled lane again. Another 100 yards, and it resumes the status of a path, with views of Minninglow in the far distance, and begins a gradual descent. Veer right, away from the wall, crossing diagonally to the right over the lower slope of the field to a stile in a facing wall which permits access to the Tissington Trail.

Turn right along the Trail, which was fashioned as a walking route by the Peak District National Park following the fall of Dr. Beeching's celebrated axe on the line from Ashbourne to Parsley Hay where it formed a junction with the Cromford and High Peak Railway.

As you stride out, notice that many of the fields in the vicinity are separated by hedgerows rather than walls, a sure indicator that you are close to the southern limits of the Pennines.

The Trail passes through a nature reserve owned by the Derbyshire Wildlife Trust. This has an abundance of rosebay willowherb, wild raspberries, harebells and birdsfoot trefoil. These attract a variety of butterflies including large and small white and small tortoiseshell.

Continue along the Trail, until you reach the car park in Tissington.

Tissington Trail, near Parsley Hay.

19. The Plague Village

A strenuous route along field and moorland paths with several steep climbs.

Route: Eyam – Sir William Hill – Eyam Moor – Leam Lane – Stoke Ford – Bretton – Eyam

Distance: 8 miles

Start: Car park, Eyam. Map reference 216767

Map: "The Peak District, White Peak Area", Number 24 in the Ordnance Survey's Outdoor Leisure series.

By Bus: There are daily services, including Sundays, from Sheffield, Buxton, Chesterfield, Stockport and Manchester.

By Car: Eyam is half a mile north of the A623, from which it is signed.

Refreshments: There are several cafes and pubs in Eyam. "The Barrel Inn", Bretton, also serves bar food.

The Plague

Plague Cottages, a row of three, stand in the main street of Eyam, not far from the church, In 1665, the middle one was occupied by a widow, Mary Cooper. In August of that year she took in a lodger, George Viccars, a travelling tailor by trade. Shortly afterwards, he received a chest of clothes from London, then in the grip of the plague. On opening the lid, he discovered that the clothes were damp so he hung them up to air.

Before long he was ill, his symptoms those of the plague. Within days, he was dead. The disease soon spread through the village and, after a short respite during the winter, appeared again in the summer of 1666 with even greater ferocity.

By then some people had fled but those who remained, led by the vicar, William Mompesson, and a former vicar, Thomas Stanley, agreed to a self-imposed quarantine. Nobody was to leave Eyam.

Food and other provisions were supplied from outside, deposits being left at certain pre-arranged spots on the parish boundary. Much was provided by the Duke of Devonshire at his own expense. The church was closed and services held in Cucklet Delph, a natural amphitheatre to the south. Today a Thanksgiving Service is held in the Delph every year on the last Sunday in August. The final victim died in November, 1666, bringing the total to 260 out of a village population variously estimated at between 300 and 700. Apart from Cucklett Delph and Plague Cottages, there are other reminders of the plague to be found in Eyam.

Mompesson's wife was a victim and her tomb may still be seen in the churchyard. However, very few were buried there. Most were simply interred in holes on their own farms or in their gardens. The Riley Graves, in a walled enclosure to the east of Eyam, present a very moving reminder of the sufferings of the Hancock family.

Riley Graves, Eyam.

Eyam Church

Apart from its associations with the Plague, Eyam Church is worth a visit. Although its age is unknown, parts of it date back to at least the twelfth century although there may have been an earlier church there from Saxon times. The pulpit is Jacobean, being the one used by Mompesson, as is the chair in the corner to the right of the altar. The Plague Register, copied from the Parish Register, is on view in the south aisle.

On the exterior of the south wall is a most unusual sundial. Made by William Shaw, a local stonemason, in 1775, it shows the time in half-hours. In addition, it carries the signs of the Zodiac and gives the local times of places in different parts of the world including Mecca, Rome and Bermuda.

Eyam Church

Eyam Hall

Eyam Hall, in the centre of the village, was built in 1671 and has been in the possession of the Wright family ever since. In summer it is open to the public.

Eyam Village

Although it is the plague story which attracts visitors to Eyam, it has a long history. For centuries, it has been associated with both the lead mining and quarrying industries. Fluorspar extraction is still important. During the eighteenth century cotton mills appeared and later silk was manufactured to be replaced later by the shoe industry. These were exported to all parts of the world, but the last pair of shoes was made in 1979.

Eyam Hall

The Walk

Leaving the car park by the main entrance, turn left into Hawkhill Road, noticing the Hall Hill Troughs on your right as you descend to the road junction. Turn left along the main village street to pass through the Square with its stocks, market hall and iron ring for bull baiting. Keep Plague Cottages on your left to reach the church. At the far end of the churchyard turn left along a signed footpath which stays just inside the eastern boundary to a metal kissing gate and an intersection in the path system.

Continue forward as the broad track traverses rough ground before narrowing to stay to the left of a stone wall. After the first stile, keep a wall on your right, following this round to the right as it corners to a stone step stile. Then make a left turn up a stepped path to another stile alongside a locked green gate which gives access to a road. Ignoring the sign to Mompesson's Well, turn left along the road for ten yards, before forking to the right up a flight of eight steps to a stile.

Plague Cottages, Eyam.

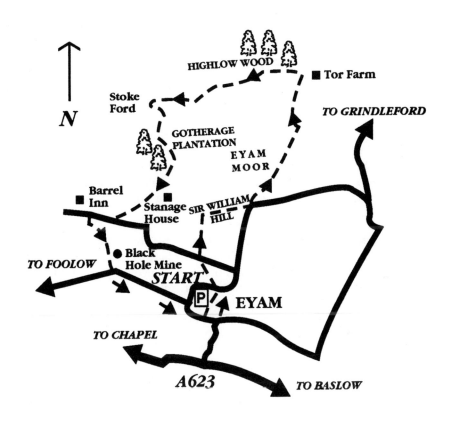

Follow the waymarked path as it climbs very steeply through the woods, clothing the flank of Eyam Edge. Great care is needed, especially after wet weather, when it can be very slippery.

In due course, a wall appears on your left. Turn left over a stile and, veering to the right, cross a succession of fields on a distinct path, using the stiles as your guide. On gaining the Eyam to Bretton road, turn left for 20 yards before making a right turn over a stone step stile. This path clings to a wall on your right as it climbs gently to pass beneath overhead wires. There is a T.V. mast close-by on your left and the chimney of Ladywash Mine on your right.

On the crest of the rise, at 429 metres, another set of overhead wires begin to run parallel to the path. With some wonderful views of the Eastern Edges, the going levels before you pass Ladywash Farm on your right. After a ladder stile turn right along a very wide walled lane as it crosses Sir William Hill and descends for half a mile to a junction with a metalled road.

Ignore a path on the left signed to Abney by the Peak and Northern Footpath Society. Advance a further ten yards to turn left along another path signed to Leam Lane. Initially, there is a fence on your right. To the left Eyam Moor is carpeted in heather while the panoramic view embraces Grindleford, Carl Wark and Higger Tor. Meadow pippits, skylarks, starlings in great flocks, crows and grouse are abundant.

After some distance, the path swings round to the left, eventually passing two solitary gateposts before swinging even further to the left and descending to a step stile by Leam Lane, opposite a farm.

Turn left, to pass both Leam Farm and Leam Farm campsite, beyond which the lane becomes surfaced. It bends sharply to the left and descends steeply for almost a quarter of a mile, before bending equally sharply to the right. There turn left onto a broad track to a five-barred gate close by Torr Farm which is on your right. Maintain the line of direction over a large field with a wall to your right. Through the next five-barred gate continue through a new plantation and then to the left of Highlow Plantation to a stile.

At the next Y-junction, fork left onto a narrower but distinct path to a stile which is accompanied by a Peak and Northern Footpath Society sign which reads, "via Stoke Ford to Abney". From there, veer to the left, up a broader track climbing through the trees for a quarter of a mile before emerging into more open country.

Continue forward, losing height gradually to pass through two gateposts and cross a stream. Climb slightly before the final descent to Stoke Ford. This is one of the most delightful spots in the National Park, a quiet haven in which to pause and contemplate. Do not cross the footbridge. As directed by another Peak and Northern Footpath Society sign, turn sharp left to climb steeply away from Highlow Brook.

After 15 yards, fork left again for an equally steep climb through the bracken as the path develops into a broader track. After crossing open ground a wall comes in from your left. Stay to the right of this with some excellent views down into Bretton Clough.

Beyond a ladder stile traverse a grass terrace to a stile by a five-barred gate. Stay to the left of the wall for 20 yards before forking to the right although still keeping to the left of the wall.

Gotherage Plantation is soon passed. Beyond, make a right turn over a stone step stile adjacent to a five-barred gate. Advance to the left of another wall but, after 100 yards, and by a gateway on your right, turn left, to pass a group of dead trees on your right.

Beyond the next step stile, advance between two walls, with Stanage House a little way off to your left, before crossing a large field with a stone barn and a group of Rhododendron on your immediate right. The next ladder stile provides access to a bridleway. Cross directly into a walled lane which leads to the Eyam to Bretton road on the crest of Eyam ridge.

Turn right for a quarter of a mile. 100 yards before reaching "The Barrel Inn" turn left over a stile by a finger post. Stay to the left of a wall while descending the field but, after a stile, veer towards the left through the gorse to reach a squeezer stile by a lane. Turn left along the lane to the Black Hole Mine. There turn right and then left and, opposite some bays, turn right again to pass through the works.

On reaching a small pond on your right, veer slightly to the left and follow the approach driveway until meeting with the Eyam to Foolow road. Turn left for the short distance back into Eyam.

20. Bakewell

A moderate walk along field paths, trails and riverside paths.

Route: Bakewell – Monsal Trail – Little Longstone – Monsal Head – Ashford-in-the Water – Bakewell.

Distance: 8 1/2 miles.

Start: Granby Road car park, Bakewell. Map Reference 219684

Map: "The Peak District, White Peak Area", number 24 in the Ordnance Survey's Outdoor Leisure series.

By Bus: There are daily buses, including Sundays, from Ashbourne, Buxton, Castleton, Manchester, Sheffield, Chesterfield, Derby, Matlock and Nottingham. There are services on summer Sundays and Bank Holidays from Barnsley, Rochdale, Oldham, Glossop and Hanley. A network of local routes from Bakewell serves local villages.

By Car: Bakewell is located on the A6 road between Buxton and Matlock.

Refreshments: There are a wide selection of cafes, restaurants and pubs in Bakewell. There is also a hotel and cafes at Monsal Head and Ashford.

Bakewell

With a resident population of 4,000, Bakewell is the only town within the Peak District National Park. The Park's headquarters are also located there.

Situated on the River Wye, it is surrounded by hills on three sides. To the east verdant, lush meadows flank the river in the direction of Rowsley. The earliest known fact about Bakewell is the existence of an Iron Age fort on a hill near Ball Cross. Far less certain is the presence of a Roman encampment. The name is of Saxon origin, appearing in several documents in different forms such as "Bad Kwell" or "Bauckwell". It is generally taken to mean "Badeca's Spring".

Bakewell Church.

Although not proven, there is some evidence that King Edward the Elder built a castle on what is now known as Castle Hill, but what is more certain is that Bakewell was a Royal Manor in Norman times. It was held by William Peverel, but subsequently passed into the ownership of the Rutland family. It has long been a centre for trade, a tradition still maintained by its large Monday cattle market. The seventeenth century Market Hall, now with windows instead of open arches, is the Peak Park Information Centre.

Bakewell Church

Bakewell parish church, dedicated to All Saints, overlooks the town. There is evidence to suggest that perhaps a Saxon building stood on the same site. Just inside the porch is a fascinating collection of carved stones, some of them Saxon. Inside, there is a monument to Dorothy Vernon and John Manners who are said to have eloped from Haddon Hall.

Other Buildings

In 1777, Arkwright set up Lumford Mill to the north of the town. Above the church, the Old House Museum occupies a Tudor building which has some wattle and daub walls still exposed. Below the church is the Old Town Hall, built in 1684. The main town bridge, much altered and widened over the centuries, was constructed in the fourteenth century, while further along the Wye is an old packhorse bridge, dating from 1664.

Bakewell Pudding

The Bakewell Pudding, not tart, was born in the kitchens of "The Rutland Arms", a hotel where Jane Austen once stayed and which she used as a setting in her novel, "Pride and Prejudice". The Pudding was a misbegotten creature that went on to win world-wide fame and popularity.

The original was the result of a misunderstanding on the part of the cook. The mistress explained that she wanted an egg mixture to be included in the pastry for a strawberry tart. However, in the event, the cook forgot her instructions and poured the egg mixture over the jam.

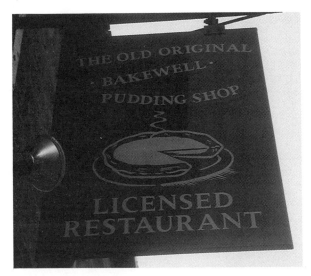

The Pudding Shop, Bakewell.

But, rather than showing disapproval, the guests congratulated the mistress who told her cook to continue making them in the same way.

Ashford-in-the-Water

Ashford is best known for its Sheepwash Bridge spanning the River Wye which has a small sheepfold

Sheepwash Bridge, Ashford.

adjacent. Every year the annual custom of washing sheep in the water is maintained.

Amongst the items in the church are "The Maidens' Crants", garlands carried at the funerals of unmarried women or girls and suspended over the family pews afterwards. The last was used in 1801. The village was once famous for its "marble", a local stone used as an inlay in Victorian times. Part of the church floor is made from it.

Ashford Church.

The Walk

From the car park in Granby Road walk through the Cattle Market and, keeping the toilet block on your right, reach the bank of the River Wye. Turn left, soon reaching Bridge Street, the A 619. Turn right over the road bridge. At the far end make a left turn through a small gate to follow the riverside path as it passes through a white kissing gate,

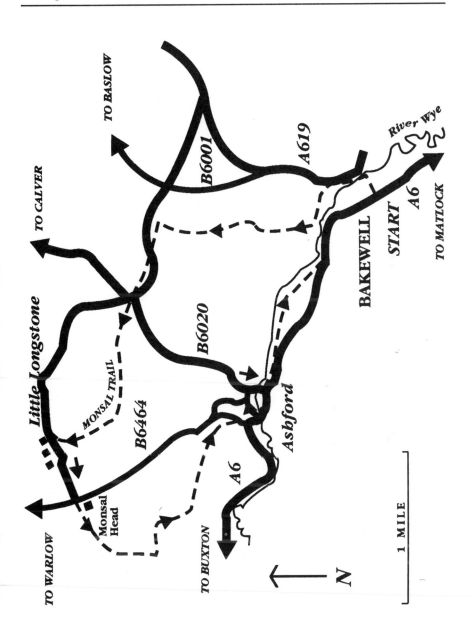

followed by a second, non-white one, after 20 yards. Proceed over the next field to a small wooden gate. Turn left along the road. After 200 yards, and by a house called "Wynfield" and the packhorse bridge to the left, turn right into a lane boasting a sign, "Smith's Runners Ltd". After only a few yards the lane curves round to the left to pass behind Lumford Cottage and embark on a climb, passing a former quarry on your right which now boasts an industrial unit.

Beyond a five-barred metal gate, the gradient eases and the countryside opens-up. Where the stoney track bends sharply to the left to pass between two obvious spoil heaps, stay forward along a broad green grassy track, quickly passing a small pond on your left. Over the next stile the track becomes a walled lane. After another stile and then a gateway, the walled lane ends but the path continues forward as it clings to a drystone wall on the right and descends gradually through a very long field where, in summer, poppies proliferate.

The lane resumes after another five-barred gate but this time with a fence on the left and a wall only on the right. Through two more five-barred gates, separated by no more than two yards, the lane acquires a wall on both sides. Ahead the A6260 comes into sight, but this is not for us. Before reaching it, the path passes through a small gate. Through this make a left turn onto the Monsal Trail, the former railway line which once carried express trains from Manchester to London along what was known as "The Scenic Route".

Stay with the Trail for more than a mile until, after Great Longstone station, now a private residence, the route is blocked by a tunnel. In accordance with the notice and waymark, turn right over a stile and then, immediately turn left along the left-hand side of a field to reach a stile. Over that, head for a gateway and a further stile and stay to the right of a wall. Where this ends, continue forward across the centre of a large field, the path being very distinct.

Over the next step stile, alongside a gate, turn left along the road, climbing gradually through the attractive village of Little Longstone to reach Monsal Head with its breathtaking views down into the valley.

Cross the B6465 and, keeping the Monsal Head Hotel on your left, go forward to the nearest corner which is by the Monsal View Cafe. Pass through the squeezer stile, studying the signs very carefully. Descend a couple of stone steps, ignoring the very first path on your left. Take the second path on the left, but avoid the one signed to "The Monsal Trail and Viaduct".

Your path is very narrow but is instantly recognised because it does not lose height through the trees. In fact, it climbs slightly to a stile after 100 yards. Beyond this the path leaves the trees, emerging onto open ground high above the valley. Soon it is running to the right of a wall and widens into a much broader green swathe, climbing even higher above the valley.

After half a mile, swing left, as directed by a waymark, towards a five-barred gate with a ladder stile alongside. Over this, the route is along a walled lane from which it is easy to see the field pattern of this upland limestone plateau. After passing through a squeezer stile by some iron railings continue across a small field for 50 yards before turning left over the stile in the corner, to start a gradual descent through another field keeping just to the left of a wall.

At the bottom of the field are two five-barred gates adjacent to each other. Negotiate the stile to the right-hand side of both gates to enter another walled lane which winds its way downhill gradually to reach Highfield Farm on the outskirts of Ashford-in-the-Water. By the farm turn right down the road, continuing until reaching the Sheepwash Bridge. There, turn left and, keeping the church on your left, walk through the village to the A6020.

Cross directly into a gated road with a cricket ground on your left. Cross two bridges to the A6. Turn left for 40 yards and then left again through a kissing gate with a sign pointing to Bakewell.

This path wends its way through riverside pastures with the Wye on the left and undulating gently through three stiles. After a fourth, stay with the path between the houses to reach Lakeside, an estate road. Cross directly into another fenced path to a stile. Continue over the field and, when faced with wire, swing left to a squeezer stile to regain the A6. Turn left along the road for the final stretch into Bakewell.

By the traffic island turn left into Rutland Square and, beyond the Pudding Shop, right into Water Lane to the car park.

21. Drowned Villages and Dam Busters

A moderate route along well-defined moorland paths.

Route: Fairholmes – Derwent Lane Head – Dike Low – Lost Lad – Sheepfold Clough – Abbey Brook – Fairholmes.

Distance: 9 $1/2$ miles

Start: Fairholmes car park, Derwent Valley. Map Reference 174894

Map: "The Peak District, Dark Peak Area", Number 1 in the Ordnance Survey's Outdoor Leisure series.

By Bus: There is no regular weekday service. On summer Sundays and Bank Holidays there are buses from Coal Aston, Chesterfield, Sheffield, Stockport, Hyde, Glossop, Barnsley, Rochdale, Castleton, Buxton and Bakewell. On summer Sundays and Bank Holidays a mini-bus service operates between Fairholmes and King's Tree at half hourly intervals.

By Car: Fairholmes car park is reached by the minor road which runs northwards from the A57. It is signed from its junction by Ashopton Viaduct.

Refreshments: The kiosk at Fairholmes serves light refreshments and drinks. Open daily during the summer and winter weekends.

Derwent and Ashopton

Today the Derwent Valley is dominated by its reservoirs. For many visitors they are the principal attraction, cradled as they are by high, rolling moors. At the dawn of the twentieth century, however, the only water to be seen there was the Derwent and its tributaries. The first of the reservoirs to be constructed was Howden, between 1901 and 1912, followed between 1902 and 1916 by Derwent.

To facilitate the movement of materials a special railway line was constructed from the main line in the Hope Valley. Part of this track is now used for the road which leads from the A57 to Fairholmes.

The biggest impact on the area resulted from the building of the Ladybower Reservoir, work commencing in 1935 and ending in 1943. Two villages, Derwent and Ashopton, were drowned. Derwent Hall, a splendid mansion dating from 1672 and subsequently a Youth Hostel, was demolished before the flooding, as was the parish church of St. John and St. James. On a more macabre note, the bodies buried in the churchyard, were exhumed and re-interred at Bamford. The ancient packhorse bridge which spanned the Derwent close to the Hall was dismantled stone by stone to be re-erected at Slippery Stones, where it may still be seen.

Ashopton village stood more or less on the site now occupied by the viaduct which carries the A57 across Ladybower Reservoir. It, too, was evacuated, and its Methodist Chapel and other buildings partially demolished before the waters came flooding in.

Ladybower Reservoir with Ashopton Viaduct in the distance.

Ladybower Reservoir from Win Hill Pike.

The Dambusters

The Upper Derwent Valley, and Derwent Reservoir in particular, was selected as the training ground for the famous Dambusters, Squadron 617, because the terrain was similar to that surrounding the Mohne Dams in the Ruhr Valley.

Tip

By the roadside close by the impounding wall of Derwent Reservoir is a small stone memorial to Tip, the sheepdog which remained by his master's side for 15 weeks after he had died in a blizzard on the moors.

The Walk

Leave the car park at Fairholmes on the signed path near the Rangers' Office. This reaches a minor road after 100 yards. The road is virtually traffic-free, being accessible only to residents and estate workers.

Derwent Reservoir.

Turn right along the road as it passes beneath the towering stone retaining wall of Derwent Reservoir, before curving round to the right and climbing gently in a southern direction. Pass to the left of Jubilee Cottage and, a short distance beyond, to the right of Old House Farm which belongs to the National Trust.

100 yards beyond the Old School on your left, and by a footpath sign, turn left into a track which reaches a five-barred gate after 10 yards. Beyond, the track swings left to pass between the ruined buildings of Well Head Farm to reach a stile. Continue forward, climbing a narrow clough or shallow valley between banks as views of Derwent Edge on your right come into view.

15 yards beyond the third stile a Y-junction is reached. Fork left, as waymarked, soon picking up the remnants of a drystone wall and a small deciduous wood on your right. After a fourth stile continue upwards to pass Lane Head Farm, with its National Trust notice, on your left.

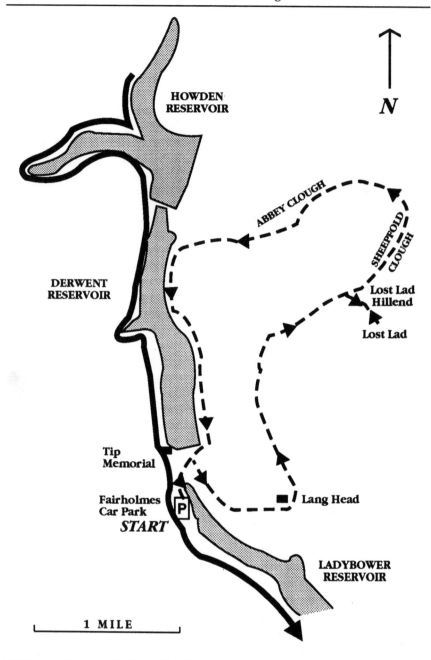

HOWDEN
RESERVOIR

N

ABBEY CLOUGH

SHEEPFOLD
CLOUGH

DERWENT
RESERVOIR

Lost Lad
Hillend

Lost Lad

Tip
Memorial

Fairholmes
Car Park
START

P

Lang Head

LADYBOWER
RESERVOIR

1 MILE

At the junction on the far side of the gate go left, still following the track uphill with a fine view of Ladybower Reservoir and Ashopton Viaduct in the distance. On reaching a footpath sign, turn diagonally to the right to double five-barred gates with a ladder stile alongside. Then bear left with the path to an obvious footpath sign on the crest of the slope.

Turn right, as signed, to walk with a wall on your immediate right. You will soon pass to the left of Pike Low, an ancient burial mound. The going is fairly level as the path traverses heather-covered moorlands.

100 yards before reaching a plantation on your right, swing to the left, as signed, soon reaching a wall gap with another footpath sign alongside. Stay forward across open moorland. At the next signed junction, fork right along the path leading towards Derwent Edge. After passing through the next derelict wall, the path passes alongside number 4 in a row of well-maintained grouse butts.

Beyond the next derelict wall, with a shake-hole nearby, stay with the path as it heads off towards the right. Within 100 yards a Y-junction is reached. Fork right. At a second junction, after a further 100 yards, fork right again through another broken wall.

Soon the path veers round to the right before climbing the slope to Lost Lad Hill End. Almost on the summit is a Y-junction. Fork right for a further short climb to the summit of Lost Lad itself, recognised by the viewfinder.

From here, on a clear day, many of the landmarks of the northern Peak District may be seen including Bleaklow, the Great Ridge, the entire sweep of rolling moorlands around the head of the Derwent Valley and beyond – even into Yorkshire. On many days, there is nothing to see but swirling mist. From the viewfinder, retrace your steps to the Y-junction. Go right to reach a stone cairn alongside a cross-roads in the path system.

Turn right for the gradual descent into Sheepfold Clough which creates the impression of remoteness and solitude. It is one of the most rewarding spots in the Peak District.

Eventually the path swings round to the left to start a steeper descent with a stream below on the right, gurgling as it cascades over a minuscule waterfall. It is an area inhabited by meadow pippit, grey wagtail and wheatear.

By Berristor's Tor the path runs to the left of some large mounds and then swings to the left as it passes a confluence of streams to enter Abbey Clough, with a view of Howden Edge directly above to your right. On its way down the valley the path crosses a succession of side cloughs, including Gravey and Cogman. At one point the path moves away from Abbey Brook before dropping steeply into a side valley to cross a stream by stepping stones, a feature shown on the map as a ford.

A short distance to your left, up the side valley, are the crumbling remains of a former building, probably a barn. Climb from the stepping stones as the path reverts closer to Abbey Brook. Finally open country is left behind as a ladder stile is reached. Stay forward to walk to the left of a combined stone wall and wire fence.

The lower slopes of the clough are wooded with a mixture of rowan, silver birch and coniferous trees. At a junction, go right, pass through a gateway and lose height rapidly to meet the bridleway which runs along the eastern side of Derwent Reservoir. Turn left.

Follow this for almost two miles. By the eastern tower of Derwent Reservoir, take the stile on your right onto a broad path down through the trees to regain the minor road. Turn right along the road to regain Fairholmes car park.

22. Mass Trespass

A strenuous moorland walk which should not be attempted in bad weather or misty conditions.

Route: Bowden Bridge – Tunstead Clough – Edale Cross – South Head – Bowden Bridge.

Distance: 7 miles

Start: Bowden Bridge car park, Hayfield. Map Reference 049870.

Map: "The Peak District, Dark Peak Area", number 1 in the Ordnance Survey's Outdoor Leisure series.

By Bus: Hayfield, one mile from the start, is served by buses from Stockport, Manchester, Glossop, Buxton, Chesterfield and Huddersfield.

By Car: Bowden Bridge car park is approached from Hayfield village along Kinder Road.

Refreshments: None on route but there is a selection of pubs and cafes in Hayfield.

The Mass Trespass

In 1932, a well-publicised ramble was organised by Benny Rothman. Its aim was to walk along the Snake Path up William Clough, which was legal, but then to spread out over the moors which was illegal. Rothman was not a member of the Ramblers' Association, or the Ramblers' Federation as it was then known. He belonged to the British Workers' Sports Federation which had close links with the Communist Party. On the appointed day, the ramblers met in Hayfield and were addressed by Rothman in Bowden Bridge Quarry before setting off to

Memorial, Bowden Bridge Quarry

William Clough. The gamekeepers were waiting for them. Skirmishes took place and subsequently, some arrests were made. Rothman and several others were gaoled for "incitement to cause a riotous assembly". The National Council of Ramblers' Federations did not support the trespass, believing that it would put back the cause of access. In 1982, a special commemorative plaque was unveiled in Bowden Bridge Quarry.

The Walk

From the car park, cross directly into the bridleway opposite which is signed "Edale via Jacob's Ladder". At the outset, this is surfaced. Once over Bowden Bridge, and with the campsite entrance on your right, turn left with the bridleway and, after a further 200 yards, follow it round through a right turn.

Climb gradually with a small river on your left. After another 250 yards, where the bridleway corners to the right over a stone bridge, stay forward into the approach to Tunstead Clough House which is signed as a public footpath.

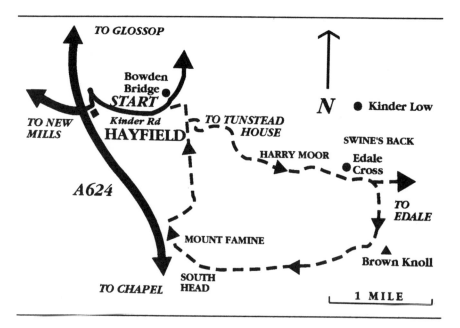

The rough track begins a steeper climb, rounding an acute bend to the right after about 50 yards. Immediately before Tunstead Clough House, turn right onto a path indicated by a crudely painted sign on a stone.

Still climbing, pass the house on your left to a kissing gate adjacent to a National Trust sign. Climb a large, sloping field, keeping to the right of a wall. Maintain the line of direction over the next stile but now more-or-less across the centre of a field to a five-barred gate with a stone step stile on one side and a wooden stile on the other. Take your choice but, once over, turn sharp right, as directed by a finger post, to walk to the left of a wall before finally veering slightly left across the field corner to a stile. Then veer further left to another stile, but ignore a National Trust sign showing a path to the right. Continue forward across another field to an obvious footpath sign pointing the way to "Kinderlow End".

Stay with the clearly defined path as it levels-out and gradually sweeps round to the left with a splendid view of Kinder Low ahead and of Mount Famine and South Head to your right.

Edale Cross

Ford a small stream, negotiate a very tall ladder stile and climb steeply again before the gradient eases as the path contours the hillside to meet a bridleway. Turn left, negotiate another stream and embark on the final climb to reach Edale Cross. Continue along this ancient bridleway and packhorse route as it descends sharply before levelling to reach a gate with a stile alongside. This is the junction with the Pennine Way, recognised by the sign.

Here you part company with the bridleway. Do not go over the stile. Turn sharp right onto the path which has a stone wall on its immediate left. There are splendid views of Swine's Back and the gritstone edges above the Edale Valley with such landmarks as Noe Stool and the Wool Packs prominent.

After a quarter of a mile along the path, climb a stile and turn sharp right, walking to the left of a derelict wall. After a further quarter of a mile a Y-junction is reached. Turn right immediately, walking to the left of a derelict wall to a Y-junction after a quarter of a mile, Fork right, staying alongside the wall and fence to pass through a very shallow valley. The walking is over fine, open moorland, but soon there are clear views down to Chapel-en-le-Frith, the White Peak and even Fernilee Reservoir in the Goyt Valley. At times the path becomes rather indistinct, so stay immediately to the left of the wall but, after a stretch of wire fence without any wall, and just before the wall re-starts, climb over a stile on the right and turn left at once so that the general line of direction is maintained.

After a considerable distance the path veers slightly to the right to reach a wall corner before running to the right of the wall. Beyond a stile the path again becomes distinct as it heads to a T-junction with another bridleway by a Peak and Northern Footpath Society sign. Ignore the directions on this sign. Simply turn right along the bridleway to pass South Head on your left and Mount Famine on your right. To your right there is a view of your outward route.

Beyond a five-barred gate the bridleway starts to lose height as it heads towards a small gate alongside another five-barred. From this point it becomes a walled lane, soon running close to and parallel with the Hayfield to Chapel-en-le Frith road.

Where another bridleway comes in from the left, and by some dilapidated corrugated-iron buildings and a caravan, turn right onto a path indicated by another Peak and Northern Footpath Society sign. Initially the path runs between a wall on your left and a fence on your right but, beyond the first gate it is no longer enclosed. After a second gate continue forward a short distance before swinging round to the left for the start of a long, steep descent with a fine view of the western edges of Kinder Scout directly ahead.

In the valley bottom the path joins another. Turn left. The new track soon acquires a surface as it continues to lose height through another five-barred gate to reach the outward route a quarter of a mile before Bowden Bridge car park.

23. Three Shire Heads

A strenuous moorland walk but mainly on well defined paths or bridleways.

Route: Wildboarclough – Crag Hall – Cut-Thorn – Three Shires Heads – Black Clough – Danebower – Cumberland Clough – Wildboarclough.

Distance: 7 miles

Start: Clough House car park, Wildboarclough. Map Reference 988699

Map: "The Peak District, White Peak Area", Number 24 in the Ordnance Survey's Outdoor Leisure series.

By Bus: Bus from Macclesfield daily, except Saturdays and Sundays. Buses from Macclesfield and Ashbourne on Sundays and Bank Holidays all year.

By Car: Wildboarclough is signed from the A537, Macclesfield to Buxton road and the A54, Congleton to Buxton road.

Refreshments: None on the route. "The Stanley Arms" and "The Crag Inn", both nearby in Wildboarclough. Brookside cafe, Wildboarclough, opens Saturdays and Sundays only.

Three Shire Heads

Three Shire Heads, a remote spot cradled by moorlands, marks the ancient boundaries of the counties of Cheshire, Derbyshire and Staffordshire. It was not affected by the boundary changes of the 1970s. The stone packhorse bridge spanning the infant River Dane was an important junction of packhorse routes crossing the Peak District.

Wildboarclough

Now a quiet backwater, Wildboarclough, dominated by Shuttlingsloe, enjoyed an industrial boom in the eighteenth century when Clough Brook powered three textile mills. Crag Mill later made carpets which were displayed at the Great Exhibition of 1851. After the mill closed in 1858, the office block was converted into a sub-post office, reputedly the largest in England. Today, even that has gone.

Three Shire Heads.

The Walk

Clough Hose car park is located just below Shuttlingsloe, the so-called "Matterhorn of Cheshire". Leave the car park by passing to the left of Clough House Farm. By the farm entrance turn left to a T-junction after ten yards.

Turn right along the narrow road which climbs steeply for 300 yards before levelling. Keep an eye open for the crescent-shaped water trough set against the wall on your left just before reaching Crag Hall after half a mile.

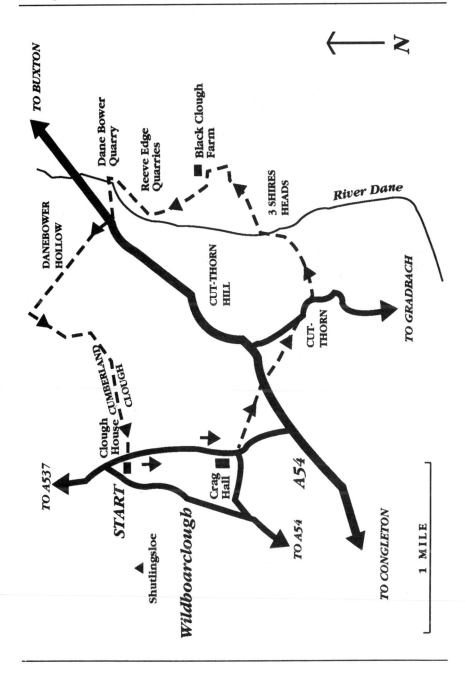

Beyond the trough another T-junction is reached. Turn left in the direction of Buxton, At first there are trees on the left and a stream below on the right. For the first 200 yards this road climbs but, where it bends away to the right, turn left into a walled lane by a Peak and Northern Footpath Society sign indicating a path to Three Shires Heads. The walled lane ends after 100 yards, a five-barred gate providing access to more open countryside.

Stay close to the wall on your left but, where this terminates, continue forward to pass a stone barn on your right before gaining the A54, Buxton to Congleton road. Cross directly to a stile with a footpath finger post adjacent pointing the way to Turn Edge.

Crossing the open moorland provides views which include the Roaches and Hen Cloud in the distance. The path, like a green ribbon, meanders across the moor and through the extensive reed patches until it meets a wall on the right. After a further 100 yards, pass to the left of Cut-Thorn house to a stile.

Turn right along a narrow surfaced road but in fewer than 10 yards, turn left into a bridleway which gradually loses height as it runs beneath Cut-Thorn Hill to reach Three Shire Heads. Immediately beyond Paniers Pool, turn right over the packhorse bridge. At the far end do not turn right again. Instead, continue forward through a metal gate to begin climbing another bridleway through Black Clough.

At the first junction fork left into a shallow valley. Pass through another five-barred gate to the entrance to the driveway leading to Black Clough Farm. Turn left over the cattle grid for a steep climb of 200 yards. Where the driveway bends, turn left through a five-barred gate, pass in front of the farmhouse and exit the premises through yet another five-barred gate.

Continue forward with a drystone wall on your left. The path soon widens as it passes through a wall gap and stays alongside the wall. Where this corners away to the left, veer right, to a gateway.

Through this turn sharp left to walk a broadening path which stays with the contour with a wall on your left. It is a good grassy path which makes for good walking.

It leads to the abandoned workings of Reeve Edge Quarry. Where the track, as it has now become, curves round to the right, stay forward along a narrower path indicated by a small post with a yellow waymark.

Pass the spoil heaps and derelict buildings before this path widens for the rapid descent to the River Dane, at this point little more than a stream.

On reaching the river turn left, as directed by another yellow waymark, cross the water by using the stones that have been deposited there and, on the far side, veer slightly to the right to climb a bank.

By the next waymark turn left for a 20 yards and scramble up some scree. At the top continue forward along a former track serving the Danebower Quarries. This climbs gradually towards a prominent stone chimney, a relic of a former coal mine on the site.

By this chimney pass through a five-barred gate and, immediately, turn sharp right onto a narrow path which climbs steeply for a short distance to a footpath finger post and the A54.

Cross directly to the bridleway sign alongside a decrepit stile and, climbing the bridleway, enjoy another moorland panorama with Axe Edge Moors to the right. After approximately a mile, another Peak and Northern Footpath sign is reached in the middle of the moors. Turn left. At first the descent over the open moorland is gradual but the gradient quickens.

On gaining a derelict stone wall stay to the right of it until a sudden, sharp drop of about 20 yards leads to the right bank of Cumberland Brook. From this point onwards the path widens until it reaches a T-junction recognised by a footpath post carrying three arms.

Turn right, soon passing through a large metal gate. The path maintains a steady descent with the tree-lined brook on your left. In autumn look out for an abundance of fungi on the ground beneath the trees.

Climb a stile next to a five-barred gate and maintain direction before turning left over a narrow wooden footbridge. At the far end turn right for the final short stretch leading to the road and Clough House car park.

24. *Arkwright's Mill*

A short walk but including two long climbs.

Route: Cromford Mill – High Peak Junction – Black Rocks – Middleton Top – Black Rocks – Cromford.

Distance: 6 miles

Start: Car park, Arkwright's Mill, Cromford. Map reference 570296

Map: "The Peak District, White Peak Area", number 24 in the Ordnance Survey's Outdoor Leisure series.

By Rail: Cromford is served by frequent trains on the Derby to Matlock line.

By Bus: Regular daily bus service, including Sundays, from Derby, Nottingham, Matlock, Bakewell, Alfreton, Manchester and Stockport. Summer Sunday buses from Congleton, Newcastle, Hanley, Chesterfield and Ilkeston.

By Car: Arkwright's Mill is about 200 yards from the A6 from which it is signed in the centre of Cromford.

Refreshments: There is a restaurant at Arkwright's Mill. There are also several pubs and cafes in Cromford village. During summer months, canned drinks and confectionery are served at Middleton Top Visitor Centre.

Arkwright's Mill

It is often thought that the Industrial Revolution was started in Lancashire, but nothing could be further from the truth. Richard Arkwright, a native of Preston, started life as a barber in Bolton, but in 1769 he invented The Water Frame, a cotton spinning machine which required water power to operate it.

Two years later, in 1771, he built his first mill in the village of Cromford in the Derwent Valley. Power was supplied by the waters of Bonsall Brook and Cromford Sough. It was the first such mill in the world and Arkwright was christened "The Father of the Factory System". He was knighted in 1786 and became High Sheriff of Derbyshire. Through this, Arkwright, became very wealthy and built Willersley Castle nearby, but this was not completed before his death in 1792. Cotton spinning stopped at the mill in 1846 and afterwards the building was used for a variety of other businesses.

In 1979, the Arkwright Society bought the site and launched a major conservation programme, parts of which are complete while others are still in progress. The mill is open to visitors daily throughout the year. Cost of admission is £1.50, with reduced rates for children and senior citizens.

Arkwright's Mill, Cromford.

Cromford Village

Prior to the arrival of Arkwright, Cromford was nothing more than a lead mining and farming hamlet. The mill owner soon changed all that.

In addition to his first mill, he built two more in Cromford, one of which, the Masson Mill, is still in operation. He also planned a model village for his workforce. Evidence of this may still be seen in the neat terraced cottages of North Street. These were built in 1777 and the following year the "Greyhound Hotel" was completed. There was even a village lock-up.

Cromford Canal

Because of poor communications in the Derwent Valley, Arkwright and other manufacturers needed to improve the situation. It was essential for the transport of both raw materials and finished products.

Arkwright was behind plans to build a canal to link Cromford with the Erewash Canal, so forming a vital link to the expanding national canal network. Completed in 1793, it cost £80,000 to build and was $14^1/_2$ miles long. With the advent of railways it declined, and was closed to all but local traffic, following the collapse of a tunnel in 1900.

Cromford and High Peak Railway

Originally, it was planned to link the Cromford Canal with the Peak Forest Canal at Whaley Bridge. Because of the number of locks required, other technical problems and the resultant financial cost, this plan was abandoned in favour of constructing a railway.

Work started in 1825 and was completed by 1830, the same year as the Stockton to Darlington was opened. Originally, horses were used to draw the trains along the level sections, while stationary steam engines hauled them up the long inclines. The horses were replaced by locomotives in 1832 but the through journey took all day to complete the 33 miles. In the later stages of its history, locomotives were employed even on the inclines.

Passenger traffic was abandoned following a serious accident, but the line continued in operation until finally closed in 1967. It was then developed as the High Peak Trail by Derbyshire County Council and the Peak District National Park.

High Peak Junction

This stands about a mile south of Cromford. The former workshops are open to the public at certain times and there are other relics of the former railway to be seen here.

Middleton Top Engine House

Middleton Top is the best preserved of all the engine houses on the Cromford and High Peak Railway. It stands at the top of the Middleton Incline which is 708 yards long and has a gradient of 1 in 8. All the machinery has been restored and on a number of days each year the engine is worked for the benefit of visitors. It is open to the public on Sundays from Easter until October and there is a small charge. The machinery is set in motion on the first weekend in every month.

The Walk

From the car park at Arkwright's Mill cross the road to the terminus of the Cromford Canal which still retains its wharfs.

Turn left by the stone warehouse and, by the corner, turn right to pass through the picnic area onto the towpath with the canal on your right. The canal runs through a broad valley with low hills sweeping up on either side. Mallard, moorhen and coot grace the water.

After a short distance the canal flows through a deciduous woodland, gaps in which permit the occasional view of the River Derwent to the left. The scene is so tranquil, it is difficult to realise that the busy A6 is only a short distance away to the right.

After one mile High Peak Junction is reached. Turn right over the swing bridge and then right again along the High Peak Trail which is signed. This begins by climbing Sheep Pasture Incline for about one mile at a

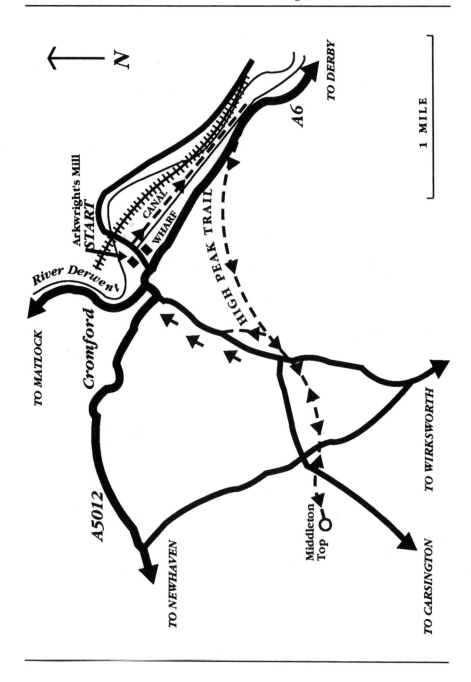

gradient of 1 in 8 as it runs through a wood. At the top, by the remains of the former engine house, there is a fine view of the lower Derwent Valley, including Willersley Castle, built by Arkwright. From the summit of Sheep Pasture Incline, the gradient levels, the High Peak Trail passing Black Rocks picnic area, Steeple Grange and the National Stone Centre, before climbing the second 1 in 8 incline to reach Middleton Top Engine House.

Because so much of the surrounding countryside in the immediate vicinity is scarred by quarries, it is best to retrace your steps to Black Rocks. There, leave the High Peak Trail by turning left through the car park and take the path which leaves the far right-hand corner. It descends rapidly through the woods.

On reaching an open, stoney area, turn left into a lane which, beyond a stile, acquires a surface for 50 yards until it meets the B5036. Turn right for the steep descent into the centre of Cromford and the A6. At the junction turn right and then immediately left into the minor road signed to Arkwright's Mill.

Wagon, High Peak Junction.

25. Two Mills

A walk through several dales with some steep climbing which is rewarded by the views.

Route: Tideswell – Tideswell Dale – Litton Mill – Water-cum Jolly Dale – Cressbrook Mill – Litton – Tideswell

Distance: 6 $1/2$ miles.

Start: Church car park, Tideswell. Map reference 152756

Map: "The Peak District, White Peak Area", Number 24 in the Ordnance Survey's outdoor Leisure series.

By Bus: Tideswell is served by daily (including Sundays) buses from Manchester, Stockport, Sheffield, Buxton, Bakewell and Chesterfield. There is a Saturday only service from Leek and Hanley. On summer Sundays and Bank Holidays there are buses from Barnsley and Rochdale.

By Car: Tideswell is about half a mile south of the A 623, Chapel-en-le-Frith to Chesterfield road from which it is signed at Lane Head junction.

Refreshments: There are several cafes and pubs serving bar food in Tideswell. There is also a cafe at Litton Mill with restricted opening.

Litton Mill

Following the success of Arkwright's first mill at Cromford, Ellis Needham built Litton Mill in 1782. It soon acquired a reputation for its harsh working conditions, especially the employment of "apprentice" child labour. In 1815, it became bankrupt and was bought by others. By 1857, it was employing 400 workers but during the 1870s was destroyed by a fire. Afterwards, it was rebuilt and in 1934 was acquired by Anglo-French Silk Mills and later turned to the production of synthetic fibres.

Today, it is closed. A scheme to convert it for use as a Time-Share complex was rejected by the Peak District National Park, a decision upheld by a Government Inspector following a Public Enquiry. At the time of writing, there is another plan to develop it for residential accommodation.

Litton Mill

Cressbrook Mill

Situated further downstream, Cressbrook Mill was built in 1815 to replace an earlier one erected on the site by Arkwright. It is a building of enormous proportions in the classical style surmounted by a cupola which houses a bell used for calling the employees to work. There is a row of cottages nearby built to house the workers who were treated more humanely than at Litton. Today, this too is empty, and is awaiting further development.

Tideswell Church

The sheer size of Tideswell's parish church has led to it being dubbed, "the Cathedral of the Peak". It also testifies to the former importance of the village which was once regarded as a market town. The nave and aisles are taller than those found in most Derbyshire churches. They are in the decorated style and work on them was interrupted by the Black Death. After that scourge work re-commenced and was virtually completed by 1370. It contains some splendid brasses and stained glass windows.

There is a splendid tomb of Sir John Foljambe and another of Sir Sampson Meverell, Knight Constable of England during the reign of king Henry VI. He is reputed to have fought in eleven battles against the French at the time of Joan of Arc. He was also Lord of the Manor of Tideswell. There was once a custom whereby local brides signed the marriage register on his tomb.

Tideswell Church.

The Walk

Leave Tideswell Church by heading south along the village street towards Town End. By the "Horse and Jockey" fork right into Gordon Road. At the crossroads just beyond the pinfold, continue forward into the lane which passes South View Farm. The lane runs parallel with, but higher than the road leading into Tideswell Dale.

On reaching a five-barred gate, a little before a galvanised metal cattle trough, fork left through an almost-obscured wooden squeezer stile, which is not signed in any way, onto a narrower path. This descends the flank of the hillside diagonally to the left until it reaches the B6049 by the sewage works.

Turn right along the road but, at the far end of the sewage works, fork left onto a maintained but unsigned path which passes through the trees to Tideswell Dale picnic site and car park. Pass through the car park, keep the toilet block on your left and take the path running down the dale. If, by this time you are feeling tired, there is the occasional bench lining the route.

Soon the steep northern slope of Hammerton Hill hoves into view directly ahead but do not worry for the path twists its way deeper into the valley, so skirting this daunting-looking obstacle. Go right over a footbridge and then left, so maintaining direction. Beyond this point the valley closes-in, the path passing through a jungle of butterbur, nettles, rosebay willowherb and deciduous trees until it meets the minor road linking Millers Dale with Litton Mill.

Turn left, reaching Litton Mill within a quarter of a mile. Continue forward along the concessionary path (the width of a narrow road) which passes through the mill complex. At the far end of the buildings, turn right over a narrow bridge and then sharp left onto a wide riverside path with the Wye on your right. The river is a succession of weirs and placid pools as it flows through a dramatic limestone gorge, the slopes of which are well wooded.

The walker is accompanied by the calls of mallard, coot, moorhen and little grebe. Notice the vast areas of walling on the railway embankments. The river widens as it enters Water-Cum-Jolly Dale, the pool having been created artificially to supply water to Cressbrook Mill.

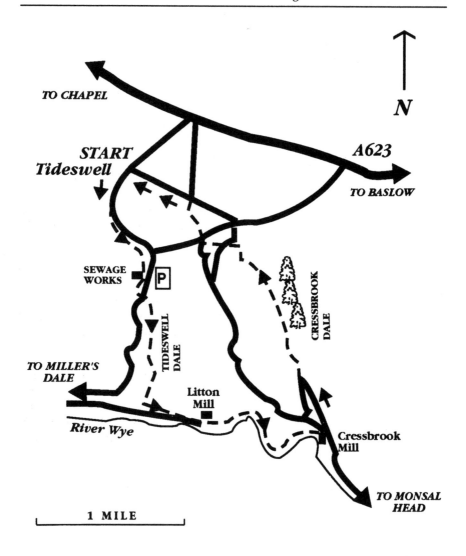

After negotiating a very tall metal kissing gate, cross a narrow footbridge and turn left through the buildings of Cressbrook Mill to reach a minor road. Turn left and then, at once, fork right into the road signposted to Cressbrook and Litton. Continue climbing very steeply to pass another road on the right leading to Ravensdale cottages. At the point where the road does a very acute turn to the left stay forward onto a broad track through the woods.

At last the going is level, but do not be too optimistic. After about 250 yards, and almost at the end of the woods, veer left onto a narrow path which climbs very steeply through the trees and, because of erosion control, has been stepped in its higher reaches. On meeting the boundary fence turn right, staying just inside the woods for a considerable distance. Through the breaks in the trees there is the occasional view across to Wardlow Hay Cop and down into Ravensdale.

On reaching a squeezer stile, turn left through the boundary before veering through 45 degrees to the right towards a stile midway along the field wall. On this section, there is a view down into Tansey Dale and the upper reaches of Ravensdale with the unusually-shaped St. Peter's Stone. Over the stile, veer left to the far corner of the second field, pass through a gateway and maintain direction to a stone step stile. Maintain the line of direction across a narrow field to a stile in the facing wall and then to another stile in the bottom of the next field. Cross directly over a narrow lane before veering left to a stile in the boundary wall of the next field.

Keep forward to the next stile which is located in the wall across the bottom of the field. Head directly up the next field to a stile giving access to a narrow lane. Turn left along this for ten yards to its junction with a minor road at a sharp bend. Turn left along the road, soon passing a barn on your left. After 100 yards, where the road curves sharply to the left, stay forward through a squeezer stile with a footpath finger post adjacent. Using the stiles as your guides, cross three fields and then, as directed by a low-placed waymarker, head for the far corner of the field.

Turn right through a gateway to reach a squeezer stile within 15 yards. This provides access to a minor road. Cross to a facing stile with 2 footpath signs. Over the stile turn sharp right, walking initially to the left of a wall. Where this veers away to your right, maintain your line of direction down a steep slope to another squeezer stile in the right-hand corner of the field. Turn right along the road for 20 yards. By "The Cottage" turn left into a green lane which climbs gradually for a quarter of a mile to reach another road. Turn left along this for the final stretch into Tideswell.

26. Spa Junction

An interesting and varied route through several dales and over sections of the limestone plateau on field paths.

Route: Wyedale car park – Blackwell Cottages – Flagdale – Wormhill – Monks Dale – Miller's Dale – Chee Dale – Wyedale car park.

Distance: 8 miles.

Start: Wyedale car park, Topley Pike, signed from the A6, 3 miles east of Buxton. Map Reference 104725

Map: "The Peak District, White Peak Area", Number 24 in the Ordnance Survey's Outdoor Leisure series.

By Bus: Daily services, including Sundays, from Manchester, Stockport, Buxton, Bakewell, Derby, Nottingham and Chesterfield.

By Car: Wyedale car park is alongside the A6 at Topley Pike, 3 miles to the east of Buxton.

Refreshments: "The Anglers' Rest" at Miller's Dale serves bar meals. At peak periods, there is also a cafe in Miller's Dale.

Miller's Dale

Miller's Dale takes its name from the corn mill for which King John granted a charter to Daniel Pincerna. No doubt replaced several times over the centuries, the last one was the building now occupied by the Staffordshire Farmers. Miller's Dale finally achieved importance as a railway junction.

Following years of railway politics a line was built through the Wye valley to allow through trains to run from Manchester to London. Miller's Dale became an important junction where passengers from London and the south changed for the final section into Buxton. It was the only railway station in England with a post office on the platform.

The line closed in 1968 and following years of negotiations it was bought by the National Park for conversion into the Monsal Trail, although the tunnel sections have been sealed off. Because he did not want his view spoiling the Duke of Rutland insisted that the line should pass under a tunnel at Haddon, and because he caught trains at Bakewell, the station was made rather more grandiose than it need have been. The Duke of Devonshire had a station built at Hassop for his own use.

James Brindley

James Brindley, the celebrated canal engineer, was born in the tiny hamlet of Tunstead which forms part of the parish of Wormhill. Today the cottage where he first saw light of day no longer stands, but the site is marked by a tiny plaque. There is a more substantial memorial to him in the centre of Wormhill which is passed on this walk.

Miller's Dale Lime Kilns

The original kilns cut out of the rock face were opened in 1880 while the massive concrete buttresses were not added until the 1920s. The kilns were worked until 1944 supplying lime to the chemical and steel industries as well as to farmers. All the coal for the burning had to be brought in by train. If you enter you will see two gritstone-lined drawing tunnels from each kiln where a man and a boy would work, drawing out the quicklime. Afterwards they would pass it through riddles to separate the lump-lime from the small-lime.

The Walk

From the car park head away from the A6, following the unsurfaced bridleway as it penetrates deeper and deeper into the steep-sided valley, wooded with rowan, beech and silver birch. The River Wye is on your left, its course marked by vast spreads of butterbur and an occasional sighting of dippers.

Beyond the third viaduct cross the narrow footbridge by Blackwell Cottages before turning right onto a narrower path, the Wye now flowing on your right.

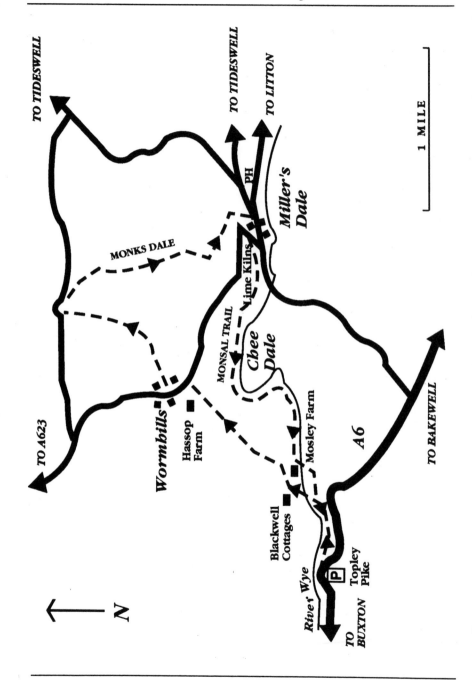

By a wall corner, fork left up a walled lane to pass under a railway bridge after 50 yards. Almost at once make an acute turn to the left and pass under overhead wires before zig-zagging up the steep hillside to Mosley Farm which is on your right.

By a gateway, turn right along the farm track, pass to the left of the farmhouse and then to the right of an outbuilding and a second house to reach a facing five-barred gate. Do not go through. Turn left along the lane, pass to the right of a plantation and negotiate a stile before all further progress is halted by a set of wooden railings.

Turn right over a not-very-conspicuous stile adjacent to a five-barred gate before aiming for a stile a few yards to the left of a telegraph pole. Maintain the line of direction over the next field to a squeezer stile before swinging to the right towards a three-armed finger post.

Do not turn. Stay forward over the stile for a steep descent on the well-trodden path into Flag Dale. Climb the equally steep path up the opposite slope. At the top of the rise, veer leftwards to pass between hawthorns to a squeezer stile.

Continue in the same direction to a gated squeezer stile followed by a second just in front of Hassop Farm. Turn right along the farm drive to reach the main road through Wormhill. Turn left along the road, passing the village stocks and Brindley's Memorial on your right, to reach a telephone kiosk. Turn right into a signed bridleway.

After the first stile, pause to admire the extensive views across the plateau of the White Peak. Where the lane is joined by another from your right, keep forward, negotiating a stile and staying with the lane as it descends through a canopy of hawthorn trees to a squeezer stile. That marks the end of the lane. Beyond stay to the left of a wall, descending very steeply to the minor road which runs across the head of Monk's Dale.

Turn right for 20 yards along this road and then right again onto the path heading over the open pasture into Monk's Dale, a National Nature Reserve. Beyond the first stile, the woods close in and the path through the dale becomes extremely rocky. Even in dry weather caution is required if a sprained ankle is to be avoided.

The path runs through this quiet, dry valley, crosses a footbridge and finally turns left behind a stone cottage with a low roof. By the far

Stocks, Wormhill.

corner, turn right to the road through Miller Dale by the Church of St. Anne. If refreshments are required, turn into the facing road, signed to Litton Mill. It is 100 yards to "The Anglers' Rest".

Otherwise, turn right along the B6049 to walk beneath a double viaduct. After a quarter of a mile turn right into the Wormhill road. After passing beneath two bridges, one of stone, the other of metal, make a left turn into the car park at Miller's Dale station.

Proceed by the station buildings, through the car park and out onto the former railway trackbed, now the Monsal Trail. After 700 yards, you will reach the lime-kilns.

One hundred yards beyond, as signed because a tunnel ahead has been sealed-off, fork right. Descend the steps. At the bottom turn right to follow the riverside path as it enters Chee Dale with its towering crags so beloved of climbers.

The path becomes very rocky and again can be treacherous after a spell of wet weather. At Wormhill Springs, cross a footbridge over a sidestream. At the far end turn right for 20 yards and then make a left turn over a second footbridge. The stream, which runs underground through Flag Dale, surges to the surface just below the second bridge.

At the far end, turn left and soon the path is using stepping stones, not to cross the Wye, but to proceed upstream beneath an enormous limestone overhang. 50 yards beyond the last of these stepping stones, turn left over a footbridge and then right to a junction after 80 yards.

Turn left along a concessionary path, initially up a flight of steps. At the top, although this may feel to be going in the wrong direction, turn left. reaching the Monsal Trail after a further 50 yards. Turn left along the Trail, passing over a bridge and under a short tunnel in quick succession.

After more than a mile, and about 100 yards beyond an arched stone bridge, fork left, as signed, descend a flight of steps and, at the bottom, turn left to follow the outward route back to Wyedale car park.

Chee Dale

27. Caudwell's Mill

A delightful walk through woodlands and across lush, upland pastures.

Route: Rowsley – Bourn's Corner – Moatless Plantation – Ballcross Farm – Bakewell Station – Calton Plantations – Calton Lees – Rowsley.

Distance: 8 $^1/_2$ miles.

Start: Car park, Caudwell's Mill, Rowsley. Map Reference 255658

Map: "The Peak District, White Peak Area", Number 24 in the Ordnance Survey's Outdoor Leisure series.

By Bus: Daily (including Sundays) services from Manchester, Stockport, Buxton, Bakewell, Matlock, Derby and Nottingham.

By Car: Rowsley is on the A6 between Bakewell and Matlock. Caudwell's Mill is signed from the village centre.

Refreshments: There is cafe serving meals and drinks at Caudwell's Mill. There is a selection of cafes and pubs serving meals in Bakewell. "The Peacock Hotel" in Rowsley also serves food.

Caudwell's Mill

It is impossible to establish the date of the first mill built on this site. However, in the 1590s there was a corn mill and a fulling mill, the latter being replaced by a saw mill during the early years of the nineteenth century. Henry Ludlam was the last operator of the corn mill and after his death in 1858 it closed, followed shortly after by the saw mill.

With a good supply of water, the site was ideally located for another mill. John Caudwell, who came from a long line of millers, leased the land from the Duke of Rutland and constructed his mill at a cost of £7,000 in 1874.

Externally it has not been altered since although the machinery has been modernised at frequent intervals. One end of the building was used for grinding provender for animal feeds, while the other produced flour. Originally it had two water wheels and 8 pairs of millstones but later power was supplied by turbines, especially after the introduction of a revolutionary new method of grinding, the roller process.

Caudwell's never developed beyond the size of a family business. At the outset they catered for a purely local market based on Bakewell and Matlock but, subsequently spread further afield, delivering to Derby, Belper and Ripley.

There was also a revolution in the distribution system. In 1887 six horses, two drays, four carts and a gig were used. By 1912, the company had a steam wagon, a lorry, a car, 24 carts, four drays and eleven horses. After they supplied flour to Chatsworth during a royal visit they advertised "Caudwell's flour makes the Royal Bread".

The mill flourished beyond the Second World War after which business gradually declined. It finally closed in 1978. It then had a staff of 14, half the number employed there during its heyday. Subsequently, the

Cauldwell's Mill, Rowsley.

buildings were taken over by the Caudwell's Mill Trust which is in process of restoring it to full working order. It is open daily, 10.00 hours to 18.00 hours from 1st April to the end of October, and during the winter at weekends only from 10.00 hours to 16.30 hours.

The craft centre, on the same site, is open daily throughout the year. Pre-booked groups may visit the mill itself daily throughout the year.

The Walk

Walk to the car park entrance. Turn left along the road to its junction with the A6 after about 200 yards. Cross the A6 into the narrow road signed as a cul-de-sac, just to the left of "The Peacock Hotel".

Pass the post office on your left and St. Katherine's Church on your right. After the church, the climbing begins in earnest. With the last house the metalled surface terminates as the road degenerates into a rough track, hedged on both sides.

By Bourn's Corner follow the lane round to a five-barred gate before entering mixed woodlands. From that point, the wide bridleway with a compacted earth surface makes for excellent walking with level going.

After a further quarter of a mile, climb again to emerge from the woodlands for an excellent panoramic view over the Derwent Valley. 15 yards before a stone gateway a T-junction is reached. Turn right to begin climbing again through Rowsley Moor Woodlands with a wall on your left. At the next T-junction, after about 400 yards, turn left along another track with an almost level gradient.

Within a quarter of a mile, the track is joined by another coming in from your left. 200 yards beyond this junction a Y-junction is reached. Fork right in the direction indicated by a blue arrow on a tree. The track climbs steeply before levelling to run through a sea of bracken which almost obscures the wall on your right. The path curves to the right, through a gateway before swinging left to cross what could almost pass for a true Alpine meadow and under some overhead power lines.

By a facing five-barred gate turn right, as directed by another blue arrow. There is a wall on your left and a wood on your right. After 100

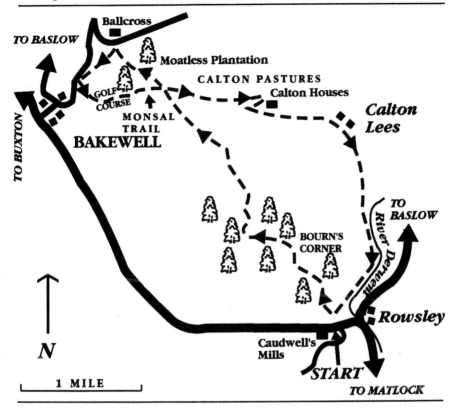

yards, climb a ladder stile. At the junction which appears immediately, fork left across the vast expanse of Calton Pastures, aiming for a small mere in the far distance. The view of the Eastern Moors, away to your right is superb, especially on a sunny day.

Keep the mere on your right to a stile in a wire fence. Fork right along the path signed to Ball Cross, staying to the left of a solitary tree while aiming for a second. By this, swing to the left up a short climb to pass to the left of Moatless Plantation.

The path, now much wider, stays along the 280 metre contour to a T-junction. Turn left. At the next junction, within 100 yards, turn left again before losing height slightly to a stile by a five-barred gate.

Stay forward to a second gate, which appears to be open permanently. The footpath finger post alongside has been broken at its base and is propped-up against a tree. Through the gate, turn left along a minor road. After 5 yards, turn left onto an unsigned path which is rather difficult to spot because of the lush vegetation.

Ball Cross Farm is opposite. Look carefully for the path entrance otherwise it could be missed very easily. There is no stile or gate.

Immediately into the trees, however, the path becomes clear and easy to follow as it descends steeply through Ball Cross Wood, given to the town of Bakewell for the enjoyment of its citizens by the Duke of Rutland. On reaching an intersection, continue forwards down the slope. The path leaves the wood to reach open country as it crosses the golf course with a fine view of Bakewell ahead.

For a short distance, it becomes a wide track but narrows again after the golf course to cross a broad track before continuing downhill to reach a road opposite a white house. Turn left along the road to a T-junction after 100 yards. Turn right into Station Road and then right into the National Park car park at the former Bakewell railway station.

Pass to the left of the station building and turn right onto the Monsal Trail, heading towards the eastern terminus at Coombes Road. However, a few yards before the second bridge, turn left up a short flight of steps to a stile.

Turn left, as signed, along a broad, green path which climbs with the golf course on your left. Over a ladder stile, cross the golf course to enter Manners Wood, also given to the town of Bakewell in the nineteenth century by the Duke of Rutland. The path develops into a wide track as it climbs. Immediately after crossing a tiny stream, fork left onto an unsigned narrower path which climbs through the trees.

At the next T-junction, by a concrete bunker, turn right for a distance of 5 yards and then make a left turn into a small valley, climbing, still very steeply, to the right of a small, square stone building. Within a few yards, a stile provides access to Calton Pastures. Turn right in the direction indicated by the waymark on the stile. Pass under some overhead wires to the right of a clump of trees to gain a stile in a wire fence.

Beyond the stile is the small mere passed on the outward journey across Calton pastures. However, the return leg is completely different. Immediately over the stile is a Y-junction. Fork left, staying just to the right of the mere, along the path signed to Chatsworth. Within 100 yards, a second stile is met with. Over that, veer right, as shown by the waymark, to cross a very large open expanse of upland meadow. Having passed through a gateway, and to the left of Calton Plantations, the path forms a T-junction with a track.

Turn right. After a short distance pass through a gate into a walled lane. Continue through the cluster of houses, Calton Lees Houses as they are marked on the map, and stay with the track as it descends down the valley which is set into a lush landscape where large white and meadow brown butterflies proliferate in summer.

At the cross-roads in the hamlet of Calton Lees, turn right. One hundred yards beyond Calton Lees Farm, turn left over a stile and then follow the path which stays very close to a fence on the left which soon becomes a wall.

By the corner of a wood, which comes down the slope on your right, climb a step stile by an oak tree. Turn right. Walk to the left of a wall and gradually move further to the left, aiming for a five-barred gate. Pass through and, taking your direction from a yellow waymark, aim for an obvious gateway. Lindop Wood is a short distance away on your right. Maintain direction across the next large field, before veering left by the fence corner to a stile.

Enter a wood. The path is very clear as it makes for a stile at the far end of the wood. Remain close to the right-hand boundary of the next field to a gateway where the path becomes very muddy in wet weather. Beyond that it develops into a track with a hedgerow on the right.

Eventually it becomes a walled lane to pass under a disused railway and through a five-barred gate. Within a further 50 yards go through large double gates and then turn left along the road into Rowsley. Cross the A6 and return to the car park.

28. Ecton Copper Mines

This route follows field paths and the track of a former light railway and involves one steep climb as it explores a section of the Manifold Valley.

Route: Hulme End – Dale Bridge – Ecton – Top of Ecton – Sugar Loaf – Wetton Mill – Swainsley – Hulme End

Distance: 6 miles

Start: National Park car park, Hulme End. Map reference 103594

Map: "The Peak District, White Peak Area", Number 24 in the Ordnance Survey's Outdoor Leisure series.

By Bus: Daily service from Buxton (train connection from Manchester), and from Leek on Mondays, Wednesdays and Saturdays. Buses from Congleton, Newcastle, Hanley, Macclesfield, Mansfield and Derby on summer Sundays and Bank Holidays.

By Car: Hulme End car park is signed from and is adjacent to the B5054 which, in turn, is signed from the A515 just north of Newhaven.

Refreshments: Light refreshments and drinks at Wetton Mill cafe. Bar meals at the Manifold Valley Hotel, Hulme End.

Ecton Copper Mines

Somewhat surprisingly the Romans, who were involved with lead mining elsewhere in the Peak District, never worked copper as they did in other parts of England. In fact the deposits there were not discovered until the eighteenth century but, afterwards, they were worked extensively making the mine the largest in Europe.

In 1786, 4,000 tons were extracted. During that century alone a profit of £1,300,000 was made. One of the largest investors was the Duke of Devonshire, so he was able to fund the building of Chatsworth and the development of the Crescent in Buxton without any real financial constraints.

Spoil Heaps and Radcliffe's Folly, Ecton Hill.

Copper mining at Ecton came to an end towards the close of the nineteenth century but the spoil heaps and other scars are still visible on Ecton Hill, although natural regeneration is helping to heal the wounds.

Some of the shafts were exceptionally deep, Ecton drawing ore from some 1,300 feet below ground. The mine even used a system of boats underground but it is worth noting that the mines were not subject to flooding.

The Manifold Light Railway

This narrow gauge railway (2 feet 6 inches) was built in 1904 with a view to carrying coal and milk to the creamery at Hulme End, and with a possibility of the copper mines re-opening at Ecton.

From the outset, it was an economic failure and lasted a mere 30 years. It ran for 8 miles through some delightful scenery from Waterhouses in the south to Hulme End where some of the former railway buildings still stand in the car park. The locomotives were unusual in that they were built to resemble some used in India, and were fitted with headlamps and cow-catchers.

Much of the track has now been converted into a surfaced walking trail although one section, between Wetton Mill and Swainsley, has been converted into the main road through the valley, leaving the original road to become little more than a track or bridleway.

The Walk

Exit the car park by heading south along the Manifold Track which has been given a macadam surface. Notice the width of the valley at this point. The grass verges are full of such wild flowers as red campion, butterbur, harebells, rosebay willowherb and ragwort. Soon, however, the valley narrows and the sides become steeper.

On reaching Dale Bridge turn left along the road from Warslow for a few yards to its junction with the main valley road. Turn right for ten yards before forking left up a metalled track with a sign indicating that it is a path to "To Top of Ecton and Wetton".

Climb steeply, passing the former sales office of Ecton Copper Mine and the Mine Agent's house before reaching Radcliffe's Folly, a house built in 1933 by Arthur Radcliffe to replace a single-storey cottage. He was Conservative MP for Leek and noted for his infrequent attendances.

Stay forward keeping to the right of the house before passing between outbuildings to a metal five-barred gate. Do not go through. Instead stay to the left to walk between two wire fences to a stile. Turn right for the long, steep climb which curves round the flank on its way to the shoulder of Ecton Hill, passing various industrial waste sites which nature, mercifully, is re-colonising.

Pause frequently to admire the view, especially from the crest of the hill where, in summer, swallows fly at the height of your head, so providing the walker with a birds-eye perspective of the valley below. The height is 363 metres.

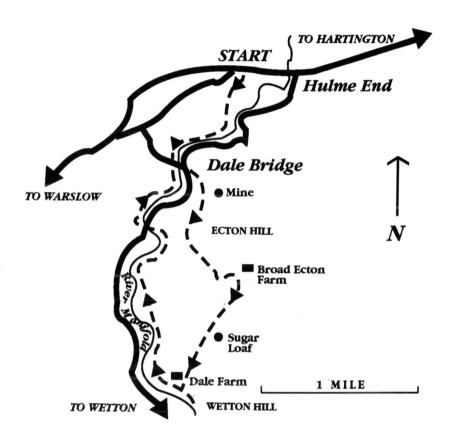

Follow the path round the shoulder to a Y-junction. Fork left but, on coming face-to-face with a solitary row of hawthorns turn sharp left for another steep but short climb to a stile. There is a fine view of Swainsley hall far below on the right. Stay forward to a gateway and, subsequently, to the far right-hand corner of the next field. There, turn right through a gateway before veering to the right along a clear path to another gateway at the end of a row of trees. Turn left and stay to the right of a wall to a five-barred gate in the left-hand corner of the field.

Keeping an eye open for the lime-kiln on the right, turn left through the gate but resume the line of direction to reach the driveway leading to Broad Ecton Farm, which is only a few yards away on your left.

Turn right along the driveway but, at the first bend, turn right again over a stile by the second of two footpath signs which are separated by no more than 10 yards. Stay to the left of a wall to commence the gradual descent into the dale. Beyond the first stile the path develops into a green track until it reaches a stile in the field corner on your left. Over this, turn right immediately and walk just around a tree to a second stile by a National Trust sign. From there, continue down a narrow, stoney gully which passes close by the formation known as ''The Sugar Loaf'', in reality a reef outcrop.

At the foot of this rather steep drop, swing right, proceeding down the valley to Dale Farm. Pass through two gates to reach the Manifold Valley at Wetton Mill of which little now remains. After refreshments, retrace the route almost as far as Dale Farm. There, turn left along a broad track signed to Hulme End. This is the former county road, unused since a section of the former railway line was converted to serve this purpose. The surface of the old road has long since deteriorated so it is now little better than a bridleway. This makes a pleasant, traffic-free alternative for the walker as it undulates gently with the River Manifold flowing on your left.

Almost towards the end of this stretch there is a good view of Swainsley Hall and its dovecote. Beyond the third five-barred gate turn left along the road, cross the bridge and turn right over a stile onto a riverside path. Having crossed the footbridge over Warslow Brook, climb gently to a gate and turn right along the Manifold Track for the last mile to Hulme End.

29. *Magpie Mine*

A fairly gentle walk along field and riverside paths with only a small amount of climbing. In summer it is a delight for botanists.

Route: Over Haddon – Magshaw Mine – Magpie Mine – Haddon Grove Farm – Lathkill Dale – Conksbury Bridge – Over Haddon.

Distance: 7 ³/₄ miles.

Start: Car park, Over Haddon village. Map Reference 203664.

Map: "The Peak District, White Peak Area", Number 24 in the Ordnance Survey's Outdoor Leisure series.

By Bus: There are services from Bakewell and Tideswell daily, except Sundays.

By Car: Minor roads leading to Over Haddon are signed from Bakewell, Ashford and Monyash.

Refreshments: Monsal Head hotel serves bar meals. Cafes in Over Haddon, including the Yew Tree opposite the car park, are open daily throughout the year except December 25th and 31st.

Magpie Mine

The remains at Magpie are the best preserved of any lead mine in Britain. It had a long but chequered history with repeated openings and closing with changes of ownership. Lead was worked there as early as 1740 but it was not until 1810 that it became profitable. In one period of four months the mine sold lead valued at £2,088 and in the two years between 1868 and 1870 lead ore worth £19,000 was brought to the surface.

Various attempts to keep the mine free of water were attempted including the installation of steam-driven pumps. One, though effective at reducing the water level, burned 300 tons of coal a month, all of which had to be transported to the site by horse and cart at an annual cost of £1,941. In a bid to combat the flooding work started in 1873 on driving a major sough or drainage channel towards the River Wye. Work was not completed until 1881 at a cost estimated variously at between £14,000 and £35,000.

The sough passed under the village of Sheldon but it interrupted the course of several springs, so affecting the water supply. To restore supplies, special water wheels had to be constructed.

There were frequent disputes over the working of veins with the miners of the neighbouring Redsoil Mine. Matters became serious in 1833, when three Redsoil miners were killed by smoke fumes created deliberately by the Magpie miners. 17 Magpie miners were charged with murder, later changed to manslaughter, but all were found not guilty. Afterwards it was said that a curse had been placed on Magpie and everyone who worked there by the three dead men.

The mine closed for the final time in the 1950s and is now cared for by Peak District National Park and the Peak District Mining Society.

Magpie Mine

Lathkill Dale

Although stretches of Lathkill Dale now form a National Nature Reserve belonging to English Nature, there are several relics to be seen from the days when this, too, was important for lead mining.

As early as 1288 there was a mention of a Mandale Mine and four years later, Leicester Abbey owned lead mines in Meadow Place Grange. By 1500, lead mining was being carried out on both sides of the dale and by 1727 two water wheels were operating. In the 1770s, the London Lead Company was extracting large quantities of ore from the valley. Mandale Mine finally went out of production in 1851. Occasional attempts to restart the workings after that date came to nothing. There are one or two mining remains to be seen upstream from Lathkill Lodge and they are passed on this walk.

The Walk

At the entrance to the car park turn left along the road, and do the same again at the T-junction after 20 yards. After 200 yards, and beyond the last house in Over Haddon, turn right over an unmarked stile onto a distinct path which keeps immediately to the right of a barn followed by a wall.

Climb gradually to a stile in the left-hand corner of the field. Turn left towards an obvious finger post with a stile alongside. By the post veer right, taking your direction from the arm of the finger post. Continue climbing gently over the rounded crest of the hill before aiming for a stone step stile some 10 yards to the left of a solitary hawthorn tree.

Veer leftwards, but stay just a little to the right of a small landfill to another stile. From there follow the distinct path diagonally left over the centre of a field, taking your direction from the left-hand side of a row of trees and another stile.

Maintain your direction to a finger post and stile. Turn right along the B 5055 for 10 yards. Turn left over a a stile partially obscured by a luxuriant growth of vegetation. Bear 45 degrees to the left towards another finger post.

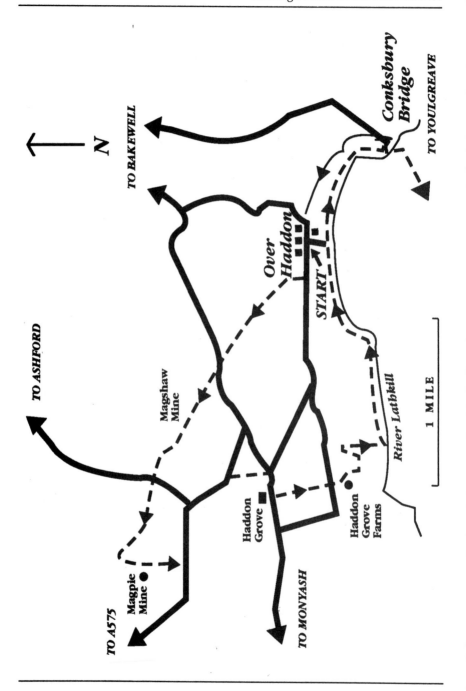

Keep the same line of direction over two stiles to a finger post in the field corner. Turn left and, keeping a wall on your right, advance to a finger post after 40 yards. Continue forward, as directed, but now to the left of a fence. After 150 yards, turn right over a stile before walking towards a very conspicuous footpath finger post 100 yards away. Be extra vigilant here. Ignore what appears to be a very distinct path. Aim for the post.

By the post, veer slightly right, as signed, to a stile by the corner of a belt of trees. Advance 10 yards before turning left over a waymarked stile to pass through a short, but wide-walled, passage. The grassed-over workings hereabouts are those of the now defunct Magshaw Mine.

Emerging from the passage, continue in a direct line down the slope to a stile adjacent to a five-barred gate. Cross the road directly into a walled lane, passing between the end of a wall and a rusting, decrepit five-barred gate. Stay forward over a broken stile next to another five-barred gate and, where the lane ends, follow the same direction but to the left of a wall.

After cresting the slight rise and walking for a short distance on the level, with the remains of Magpie Mine just ahead, turn right through a squeezer stile in the wall and then immediately turn left.

You are now to the right of the wall. Advance to the field corner. Turn left over a stile to the mine buildings. Walk by the chimney and other remains to a wide track which leaves the site by a small stone house. On reaching the road, turn left. At the junction with the Ashford road turn right in the direction signed to Bakewell. A quarter of a mile beyond this junction, part way round a bend to the left, turn right into a walled lane.

When this reaches the B5055, turn right for the short distance to Haddon Grove Farm, identified by the holiday cottage sign. Opposite, turn left over a step stile, stay to the left of a copse of trees and advance down a long field with overhead wires initially running parallel.

Where the wires turn sharply to the left, maintain your line of progress to a five-barred gate and exit onto a minor road. Turn left for 5 yards, and then turn right down the drive to Mill Farm.

On approaching the buildings, turn left, as signed, to walk between two outbuildings to a stile. This provides access to a a green walled lane which corkscrews down a long dry valley to meet the main path through Lathkill dale.

Turn left, negotiate a stile, and continue downstream for over a mile before going through two five-barred gates close together onto the minor road which terminates at Lathkill Lodge. Anyone wishing to shorten the walk should turn left along this road for the steep climb back to Over Haddon.

Otherwise, cross the road, round the corner of the Lodge so that it is on your left and enter the path signed to Conksbury. Before leaving this spot, however, look at the old stone clapper bridge spanning the dry river bed choked with butterbur and other vegetation because here the River Lathkill flows underground.

Resuming the walk, keep the river on your right for another mile to Conksbury Bridge which carries the road from Bakewell to Youlgreave. Turn left up the road for a very short distance to a tiny parking place. There, turn left through a squeezer stile to follow the distinct path through a series of stiles to the Lathkill Hotel.

Pass to the left of the pub for a glorious view and, at the next junction go left to walk along the village street to the car park.

30. Solomon's Temple

A moderate walk climbing through woodland and over moorland paths.

Route: Poole's Cavern – Solomon's Temple – Ladmanlow – Stanley Moor – Leap Edge – Dane Head – Thatch Marsh – Burbage – Poole's Cavern.

Distance: 7 $1/2$ miles.

Start: Car park, Poole's Cavern Country Park, Buxton. Map Reference 049726

Map: "The Peak District, White Peak Area", Number 24 in the Ordnance Survey's Outdoor Leisure series.

By Rail: Poole's Cavern is within easy walking distance of Buxton town centre. Buxton is served by frequent trains from Manchester, Stockport and intermediate stations.

By Bus: Poole's Cavern is served by service number 58 on Saturdays and summer Sundays. Daily (including Sundays) buses run to Buxton from Manchester, Stockport, Sheffield, Chesterfield, Derby, Nottingham, Hanley, Bakewell and Glossop.

By Car: Poole's Cavern is located in Green Lane, Buxton, and is signed from the town centre. Buxton is on the A6.

Refreshments: There is a small kiosk at Poole's Cavern. Buxton has a large selection of cafes, pubs and hotels.

Solomon's Temple

Situated high on the hills above Buxton, Solomon's Temple is an obvious landmark, especially when approaching the town from the north. Sited on a Stone-Age burial mound, it was constructed as a folly by local farmer Solomon Mycock, to provide work for the unemployed during the recession of 1896. Today, it attracts thousands of visitors who climb the steep slope of Grin Hill to enjoy the panoramic view it offers of both the Dark Peak and the White.

Solomon's Temple

Nearby is the old quarry of Grin which was worked for limestone from as early as the sixteenth century. The original ash woodland was felled during the seventeenth and eighteenth centuries, the timber being used to fire the lime-kilns.

In due course, the whole area was converted into a massive industrial tip and eye-sore which marred the image which the Duke of Devonshire wished to create for his new spa town. In 1820, he had the entire area planted with beech, lime, rowan, oak, hazel and other species which flourished to produce the mature woodland of today.

Poole's Cavern

Poole's Cavern, at the foot of Grin Hill, was described by Charles Cotton in 1680 as "The First Wonder of the Peak". Since being taken over by the

Buxton Civic Society, it has been developed as a show cave with its magnificent displays of stalactites and stalagmites.

It is named after a notorious highwayman who plagued the Peak District and used the cave to conceal his ill-gained booty. However, it has a much longer history of human occupation. Excavations have revealed that it was lived in by prehistoric man and was definitely used by people during the Roman period. Roman pottery and other artefacts unearthed during recent digs are on display in the Visitor Centre.

Poole's Cavern is open daily from Easter to the end of October between 10.00 hours and 17.00. It is closed on Wednesdays during April, May and October. Solomon's Temple is open all year.

The Walk

Exit the car park by the short flight of steps some 50 yards to the left of the Cavern Gift Shop. At the first T-junction turn left to reach a Y-junction within five yards. Fork right onto the track which climbs up the flank of Grin Hill. As the increasing light shows that open country is close at hand, fork right at a junction to a stile on the woodland boundary. Turn left onto one of the many paths leading to Solomon's temple which is clearly visible.

After climbing the stone steps to the top of the tower, retrace your steps to the stile. This time, however, do not climb over. Instead continue forward keeping to the left of a wall.

After 50 yards go through a gate to turn left immediately. Walk through a short cutting in the limestone. At the first junction beyond the cutting, turn right onto a path which leads down into the car park in the former Grin Low Quarry. Reclamation work commenced in 1979. It involved moving and levelling 500,000 cubic metres of spoil, spreading 5,000 tons of topsoil, planting 50,000 young trees and building 1,700 metres of drystone wall. Continue through the car park, passing the ranger's Office on your right, before proceeding down the entrance driveway to the road linking Harpur Hill and Ladmanlow.

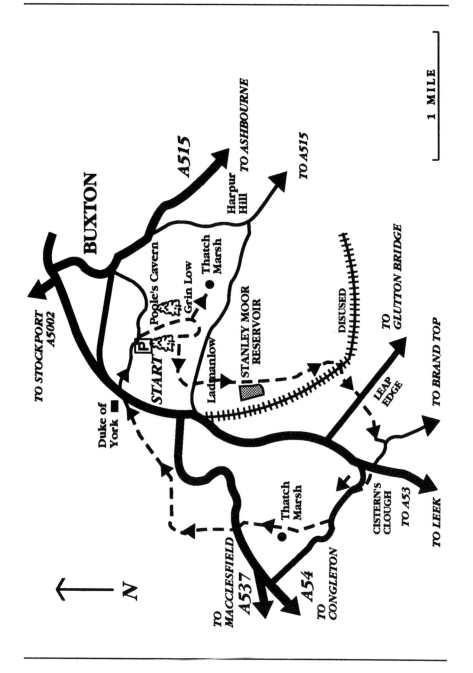

Cross directly to the lane which passes between two houses to a metal five-barred gate. This is the approach to Stanley Moor Reservoir and provides views of Axe Edge away to your right. Follow this track as it passes to the left of the reservoir.

After passing a derelict brick building, obviously a former pumping station, fork right along a broad grass path, so ignoring the main track with its chatter surface which heads off towards the left. The path keeps to the right of a wall and crosses open moorland before running alongside the track of the former Cromford and High Peak Railway.

After a while, swing right to cross this track and to reach a junction at Turncliff. Turn right to climb gently to a metal kissing gate next to a decrepit five-barred affair. Both permit access to the minor road which links Earl Sterndale with the A53. Cross directly to a stile, taking the path which initially stays to the left of a wire fence as it descends the flank of Leap Edge. At the subsequent intersection of paths, continue forward and negotiate a five-barred gate opposite a house and directly beneath some overhead wires.

Turn right along another minor road to the A53. At the junction turn right for a few yards and then turn left into the lay-by at Cistern's Clough. Where the lay-by curves sharply to the right, and by heaps of stone chippings, turn left over a stile and climb slightly for the short distance to yet another minor road. Turn left. Walk for approximately a quarter of a mile. At Dane Head, source of the River Dane, turn right by a footpath finger post onto a broad path. Signed to the Goyt Valley, it crosses a stretch of moorland to a Y-junction at Thatch Marsh. Fork left for the gradual descent to the A54, Buxton to Congleton road. Turn left for 100 yards to a small lay-by. There, turn right onto a broad, unsigned green track. Almost immediately fork right. Within yards cross directly across another path and then swing right.

At the next Y-junction fork left to the bridleway which was once the Buxton to Macclesfield Turnpike. Turn right. Stay with this bridleway to reach the outskirts of Buxton at Burbage where it acquires a surface and becomes lined with houses. At the traffic lights, cross into Macclesfield Road but, opposite "The Duke of York" public house, turn right into Duke Street. At the junction make a left turn into Green Lane which leads to Poole's Cavern and the car park.